NAIC Official Guide Introduction to Successful Investing *Handbook*

Written by Angele McQuade
for the National Association of Investors Corporation

Published by National Association of Investors Corporation (NAIC)
Madison Heights, Michigan
Copyright © 2004

First published in the United States of America by
National Association of Investors Corporation (NAIC)
711 West 13 Mile Road, Madison Heights, Michigan 48071
1-877-275-6242 • www.better-investing.org

Manufactured in the United States of America
Edition #1
ISBN # 0-9678130-2-6

McQuade, Angele.
   NAIC official guide : introduction to successful
investing handbook / written by Angele McQuade for the
National Association of Investors Corporation.
      p. cm. -- (NAIC Better Investing Educational Series)
      Includes bibliographical references and index.
      ISBN 0-9678130-2-6

      1. Investments. 2. Finance, Personal. I. National
Association of Investors Corporation. II. Title.

   HG4521.M395 2003   332.6
                    QBI03-200319

NAIC BetterInvesting Book Series

The BetterInvesting Book Series is designed to provide information and tools to help individuals and investment clubs become successful long-term investors. By using the series, investors will follow a self-learning pathway, gaining knowledge and building experience to make informed investment decisions. The series provides information and resources for beginners, intermediate and experienced investors.

For more information contact NAIC: 1-877-275-6242, or visit the NAIC Web Site: www.betterinvesting.org

Acknowledgements

NAIC OFFICIAL GUIDE – INTRODUCTION TO SUCCESSFUL INVESTING *HANDBOOK*

Author/Writer:	Angele McQuade
Executive Editor:	Jeffery Fox, CFA Director, Educational Development, NAIC
Editorial Consultant:	Barrie Borich
Index Consultant:	Kathleen Paparchontis
Educational Content Consultants:	Kenneth Janke, Chairman, NAIC Richard Holthaus, President & CEO, NAIC Thomas O'Hara, Chairman Emeritus, NAIC Donald Danko, NAIC Trustee Robert O'Hara, Vice President, Business Development, NAIC Adam Ritt, Acting Editor, *Better Investing* magazine Dennis Genord, Manager, Mutual Fund Education Amy Crane, outside consultant Laura Berkowitz, Content reviewer Ann Dexheimer, Content reviewer Judith Russ Leon, Content reviewer Nancy Isaacs, Content reviewer Betty Sinnock, Content reviewer
Creative Direction & Design:	Michael Bell Sharon Flanigan
Design Consultants:	Ellada Azariah, Graphic Designer, NAIC Pamela Forton, Graphic Designer, NAIC Mary Treppa, Online Editor, NAIC
Production Coordinators:	Renee Ross, Childers Printing & Graphics, Inc. Jonathan Strong, Director, Corporate Development, NAIC
Printing/ Production:	Childers Printing & Graphics, Inc. Printwell Acquisitions, Inc.

Table of Contents

FOREWORD — VI

INTRODUCTION — 1

PART ONE:
Getting Started — 9

CHAPTER ONE: Your Financial Foundation — 10

CHAPTER TWO: Why Invest? — 20

CHAPTER THREE: Risky Business — 28

CHAPTER FOUR: Pulling It All Together — 38

CHAPTER FIVE: Tax-Advantaged Investing — 48

PART TWO:
Investing in Stocks — 55

CHAPTER SIX: Stock Market Basics — 56

CHAPTER SEVEN: Finding Good Prospects — 62

CHAPTER EIGHT: NAIC's Stock Selection Tools — 66

CHAPTER NINE: Buying and Selling Stock — 78

PART THREE:
Investing in Mutual Funds — 87

CHAPTER TEN: Mutual Fundamentals — 88

CHAPTER ELEVEN: Finding a Place for Funds — 96

CHAPTER TWELVE: Types of Mutual Funds — 100

CHAPTER THIRTEEN: Mutual Fund Mechanics — 104

CHAPTER FOURTEEN: NAIC's Mutual Fund Tools — 108

PART FOUR:
Investment Club Basics — 113

CHAPTER FIFTEEN: Considering Club Membership — 114

CHAPTER SIXTEEN: Joining an Investment Club — 120

CHAPTER SEVENTEEN: Starting an Investment Club — 124

CHAPTER EIGHTEEN: Running an Investment Club — 132

PART FIVE:
Beyond the Basics — 137

CHAPTER NINETEEN: Turning to Your Computer — 138

CHAPTER TWENTY: Being a Responsible Investor — 150

APPENDICES

APPENDIX A: Online Resource Guide — 156

APPENDIX B: NAIC Investment Club Partnership Agreement — 157

APPENDIX C: Glossary — 160

INDEX — 171

Foreword

Getting started as an investor in common stocks is an important step to financial security. There have been countless studies made through the years that have indicated the commitment to invest is the key. A misconception is that someone must be rich to be an investor. That is simply not the case.

A great many plans are available to individuals who wish to begin with a modest investment and see it grow over the years. Whether someone wishes to organize an investment club, or start out on his or her own, it can be done. We are aware of many members who have begun with a modest amount of money and were able to see it grow to substantial figures.

What they had in common was adherence to some basic principles that NAIC has recommended

since its inception in 1951. Those principles are covered in detail in this book, but are actually quite easy to follow. Success in investing means discipline and a fundamental approach to analyzing companies and their stocks. It also means taking the long-term view when investing. Few people have been able to amass fortunes by trading stocks. The safer and more sensible approach is to buy stocks of companies that continue to grow in the future. That is what this book is about and if you read it thoroughly, you have taken an important step to financial independence.

Kenneth S. Janke
Chairman
National Association of Investors
Corporation

Introducing NAIC

The National Association of Investors Corporation (NAIC) is a non-profit, volunteer oriented, educational organization founded in 1951 to help people become successful investors. Since then, NAIC has offered investment education to over five million investors. Are you ready to join them?

Why NAIC?

NAIC's vision is to build a nation of individual investors, and its mission is to provide a program of sound investment information, education and support to help create successful lifetime investors. Whether you're experienced or just starting out, investing on your own or as part of an investment club, NAIC offers tools and resources to help you learn the skills necessary to build and maintain a profitable portfolio of stocks and mutual funds. Through its dedicated network of volunteers, NAIC presents investment classes and other educational events on the regional and the national level.

You'll find NAIC's investment principles being used in a wide variety of environments, ranging from retirement communities to workplace investment clubs to high school classes and beyond. Investors who already have all the money they'll ever need as well as those who only have $20 a month to invest can all practice NAIC methods successfully. Whoever you are, whatever your background and financial status, NAIC provides the tools and strategies that you need to become a successful investor.

Why now?

The earlier you begin to invest, the greater your portfolio can grow and the sooner you can attain your financial goals. Ideally, you should start investing as soon as you start working (or even before), but this isn't always possible. Some people grow up in families where money and investing are never discussed, and they might not realize until decades later how important investing is to their future. Others might not think they have enough money to invest, so they never bother exploring their options. Still others think the whole subject is too complicated, or they're afraid that even if they try to learn more, they'll never have enough time or will never understand enough to be able to manage their own investments.

It's true that the idea of learning to invest might be intimidating if you've never been exposed to it or feel insecure about your abilities. But the success of countless NAIC members is proof that regardless of your financial background—or lack of it—you too can learn to invest if you're willing to open your mind and put a little effort into it. Many NAIC members start the education process knowing nothing about investing or money management only to grow into confident investors after studying and using NAIC's classes, books, software and online resources.

The only thing holding you back from investment success is your own hesitation. If you have even a minimal amount of money to invest combined with the motivation to stretch your knowledge, you're on your way already.

Start your journey here

We've designed this book to be an introduction both to investing and to NAIC. By the time you're done reading it, you will have learned the basics of investing, including why you should invest, how to get started, and where to turn next for more information on your investment journey. You'll also know more about NAIC and the resources you can use to become a successful investor.

You'll find information here about investing in individual stocks and mutual funds, as well as the pros and cons of both. You'll be introduced to the basics of stock and mutual fund analysis, and you'll learn about software and other resources that can make the research process a lot easier than doing it with pen and paper. You'll even learn about investment clubs, which can be a wonderful way for beginning investors to start investing in a supportive, friendly environment.

NAIC is made up of investors at many levels of experience, from those who have never made an investment to those who have been investing successfully for decades. If you're a beginner, read through this book from the beginning to learn the basics of investing. Otherwise, you may only want to read through the sections that cover topics you're not already familiar with or those you need a refresher on.

A lifetime of learning to come

This is just the first in a series of NAIC investment education books. In other books in this new Better Investing series, you will learn how to analyze individual stocks and mutual funds, how your computer and the Internet can make investing less complicated and more efficient, how to manage your portfolio according to NAIC's common sense strategies, and how to start and run a successful investment club. Choose the subject areas that interest you most as you continue your investment education with other books in this series, and soon you'll be even farther along on your journey than you expected when you started this introductory book.

If you finish the entire series and still want to learn more, you'll be pleased to know that NAIC offers a variety of opportunities to learn about advanced investing topics. You'll find more information about these online and in-person options, including the I-Club-List and NAIC's national events, in this book and in the others in this series.

Other Better Investing books:

NAIC Stock Selection Handbook by Bonnie Biafore

NAIC Mutual Fund Handbook by Amy Crane

NAIC Investment Club Operations Handbook by Jonathan Katz

NAIC Investment Club Accounting Handbook by Richard Beaubien and Matt Stoller

NAIC Investing for Life—Youth Handbook by Fritz Williams

NAIC Computerized Investing & the Internet Handbook by Douglas Gerlach

NAIC Using Portfolio Management Wisdom Handbook by Bonnie Biafore, Beth Hamm, Peggy Schmeltz, and Betty Taylor

Making the most of this book

Throughout *NAIC's Official Guide—Introduction to Successful Investing Handbook,* you'll find explanations and definitions aimed at making you a more knowledgeable investor. To help you in this effort, we'll present certain words to you in *italic, colored* text. You'll find a definition of each of these words in the glossary near the end of this book. You'll also find an Online Resource Guide in the appendix with listings of Web sites to visit for more information on many of the subjects we introduce in this book.

We've included profiles of actual NAIC members, young and old, experienced and beginner, throughout the book. We hope their struggles and triumphs will inspire you along your own investing journey and remind you that anyone can learn to be a successful investor, regardless of who they are or when they start.

What does NAIC offer?

NAIC's educational resources center on a series of stock and mutual fund study forms and portfolio management tools, available in both paper and software versions. You'll be introduced to many of them in this book. You'll find detailed instructions for using these tools in other books in this series.

Investing tools and resources

NAIC membership carries with it many benefits. All NAIC members receive *Better Investing,* a monthly print magazine filled with the latest investment education and information, including the popular *Stock to Study* feature. Members also have access to current and past issues of *Better Investing* magazine online. Individual NAIC members and investment club members have the option to purchase a subscription to NAIC's *Online Premium Services* (OPS), a computer web based product used with NAIC software. OPS subscribers can also read the monthly online publication *BITS,* which focuses on computer-related investing. Members with OPS have unlimited access to frequently updated online data files which can be easily downloaded into NAIC stock selection and stock screening software, making stock analysis fast and convenient.

Another benefit of NAIC membership is NAIC's *Low Cost Investment Plan,* which offers an economical way for investors to build a portfolio of individual stocks with as little as $25 a month by enrolling in a company's *dividend reinvestment plan* (DRIP). NAIC members also receive discounts on NAIC software as well as national and regional classes and events.

At the center of NAIC's educational mission is a set of stock and mutual fund tools designed to help investors learn to take control of their own portfolios in an educated fashion. For decades, NAIC's *Stock Selection Guide* and other stock study tools have been the cornerstone of an investment education program that has helped millions of investors to take the mystery out of stock analysis. Now NAIC offers mutual fund study tools as well, allowing investors to create a portfolio capable of meeting all their investment needs.

If you're interested in learning how to analyze and invest in stocks and mutual funds to build your own portfolio according to your financial goals, NAIC gives you the resources to do just that. NAIC's tools are practical and well designed, something even the most inexperienced investor will appreciate. You'll learn more about these stock and mutual fund tools later in this book, and in more depth in other books in this series. You can also find classes around the country and resources online to help you make the most of these educational offerings. Millions of people find investing to be a fascinating and rewarding

activity. With NAIC's help, you can discover the excitement of taking control of your own investments as well.

Personalized learning

Over 110 NAIC regional chapters hold local educational events and classes. NAIC also offers two annual national events: *CompuFest*, three days of computer-focused investment education seminars, and the *Better Investing National Convention*, a combination of educational classes and the Corporate Expo featuring representatives from dozens of publicly traded companies. These events provide NAIC members and other interested investors an opportunity to learn more about investing while enjoying the company of others also in pursuit of investment education.

Standing up for the small investor

NAIC also acts as a voice for investors—supporting initiatives that promote investor education and opportunity. NAIC recognizes the value of providing investment education to everyone, regardless of age, gender, race or creed. NAIC works with officials at the state and national levels, with corporations and other organizations to address investor needs, advance investor education and maintain a level playing field for investors.

NAIC's four investment principles

Investing doesn't need to be complicated or confusing. Even if you don't know what a mutual fund is or why to invest in stocks in the first place, you've taken an important step by simply wanting to know more. We're not saying you'll be a stock market expert when you're done reading this book, but we're willing to bet you'll feel a lot more confident about your ability to learn the skills needed to invest on your own.

Fortunately, these skills can be learned by anyone with an open mind and a little motivation to take control of their financial future. We'll focus on teaching you to follow NAIC's four investment principles:

1. Invest a set sum of money regularly over your lifetime.

2. Reinvest earnings, dividends and profits.

3. Buy growth stocks and stock mutual funds.

4. Diversify your investments.

By applying these four investment principles in a deliberate, thoughtful way, you can begin to build a portfolio that will help you reach your own personal financial goals.

This book will introduce you to these four principles and show you how to start applying them in your life. We'll discuss why investing is so important, what

your financial goals are, how to make investing a part of your financial routine and what types of investments are best for your financial situation. Then we'll move into the details of how to invest and where to find suitable investments, ending with an introduction to stock and mutual fund analysis and how to manage your portfolio for long-term success.

The rewards of investing

By applying NAIC's four investment principles, you will increase your likelihood of finding investment success. Don't think we're offering a quick or guaranteed road to investment riches, though. To the contrary, NAIC is focused on getting rich slowly. It's true—slow and steady progress towards your financial goals may not be as exciting as trading in and out of the stock market on a daily basis. But are you looking for excitement, or are you looking for the secure

financial future and confidence that come from knowing how to build and manage your own investment portfolio?

By following NAIC's four investment principles, practiced for more than half a century by successful individuals and clubs, you can apply a consistent philosophy aimed at fulfilling your long-term investment goals. You'll learn to invest regularly, and why it doesn't matter in the long run whether the market is up or down on any given day. Putting these four simple principles into action will teach you how to identify quality companies at reasonable prices and show you how to choose quality mutual funds as well. But more than anything, they'll give you the tools and support you need to begin a disciplined, commonsense investment plan that you can take advantage of no matter what your financial background may be.

George Nicholson on NAIC History

Before we move forward and start discussing investments, let's step back in time for a brief moment and turn to George A. Nicholson, Jr. (1908-1996), a co-founder of NAIC and creator of the Stock Selection Guide, for his recollection of NAIC's birth and expansion. These comments are excerpted from his introduction to the NAIC book *Starting and Running a Profitable Investment Club.*

Investment clubs have existed in the United States for more than a century. The oldest known investment club began operations in Boston in 1882. The modern investment club movement began in Detroit in 1940. Frederick C. Russell, unable to find a job and desiring to buy a small business, decided to form an investment club as the vehicle for accumulating capital. He became the inspiration for the investment club movement.

Being a serious undertaking, the Mutual Investment Club of Detroit, at my suggestion, determined to do three things: invest every month, reinvest all dividends and buy growth companies. Each principle in itself was adopted for safety, but the three in combination produced aggressive results over the years. Having observed the Mutual Investment Club of Detroit for over 50 years, I believe it is possible for most people to achieve a goal of investing $20,000 in stock over 20 to 30 years by budgeting $20 to $25 for such a purpose.

Seeing the progress of the Mutual Investment Club and noting the ways in which the club members advanced in their family finances and businesses, we first discussed the creation of a national association in 1949. On October 20, 1951, the National Association of Investment Clubs (NAIC, now the National Association of Investors Corporation) was founded at the Rackham Building, Detroit, with the Mutual Investment Club of Detroit and three other Michigan clubs as charter members. One of NAIC's objectives was to transform investment clubs into a vast, nationwide educational project.

Having found a vigorous interest in investment club work abroad, NAIC took the lead in establishing the World Federation of Investment Clubs on July 8, 1960 in London. Investment education worldwide has been gradually broadening from its investment club base to include growing numbers of individual investors.

Taking your first step

Since its beginnings in 1951, NAIC has helped even the most novice investors learn to take control of their financial future. Throughout this book we'll return to NAIC's four investment principles and the ways you can incorporate them into your own investment plan. These four principles form the basis of an investment education with the potential of a lifetime of rewards, both financial and intellectual.

NAIC's stock and mutual fund study tools can help you learn to choose investments best suited for your portfolio. This book will introduce you to NAIC's Stock Selection Guide and mutual fund study tools, which are used by NAIC investors of every level of experience. With just a little investment of time and dedication, soon you'll be able to put these tools to work in your own portfolio.

Five million investors have taken the first steps of the journey towards investment knowledge and financial stability using NAIC's philosophy and tools. Ready to join them? Let's get started!

PART ONE:
Getting Started

Your Financial Foundation

Before You Start...

You're probably fairly interested in starting to learn about investing right away, so don't get upset when we say slow down. Before you start to invest, you need to take a close look at your entire financial picture and make sure you've taken care of some basic financial needs before you put money into your investment accounts.

Where to begin?

Are you ready to start investing? Get ready, get set, stop right there! As frustrating as it may seem, you need to take care of a few things before you commit a penny towards investing.

1 Prioritize your financial goals

The very first step you should take is to decide why you want to invest in the first place. What do you hope to learn? What will you do with your investment proceeds? How long is your investment timeline? At the end of this chapter, you'll find space to briefly answer these questions. By writing down and thinking through these financial goals, you'll create the beginnings of a plan to help you achieve them.

Without knowing what you hope to accomplish, you may find yourself losing enthusiasm for your investment education if it becomes a little harder than you expected. But if you remember that you're learning to invest so that you can buy your dream home or retire in Paris at the age of 45, you can give yourself an extra push if you get discouraged.

2 Analyze your current financial situation

Once you've set your financial goals, you'll want to take stock of where you are and how far you need to go. One way to keep track of your financial progress is to calculate your *net worth* at least once a year and maybe even every six months as you get started on your new financial journey.

What do you own?

Your net worth is simply a way of measuring your financial health. You can get very detailed and calculate it down to the penny, but you need only a rough idea for our purposes. First, add up all your *assets* (an accounting term that simply means what you own). These include bank accounts, retirement savings, any investments you own, the market value of your house and any other real estate you own and the resale value of any cars you own. Though you wouldn't be likely to sell your house and car or clean out your retirement accounts in a financial emergency, you should still count these as assets.

Because we're doing just a rough calculation, you'll probably want to leave out items such as household goods and collectible items (unless they're very valuable). If you do want a "to the penny" accounting of what you own, go for it, but we're primarily looking for a general idea of where you stand financially.

What do you owe?

Next comes the part you might prefer to avoid—your *liabilities* (a fancier word for debt). Add up your mortgage balance, credit card balances (all of them, including department store or gas cards), car loans, loans against retirement accounts, student loans, outstanding bills and any other money you might owe. Even if it's not a pretty picture, at least you now have a list of everything you owe.

Where do you stand?

Take the amount of your assets and subtract your liabilities to find your rough net worth. Are you surprised by the result? Whether it's a pleasant surprise or a wake-up call, you now know where you stand financially.

If your net worth is negative (and even if it's not), you'll probably want to set up a household budget to track where your money is going. Then you can find ways to ensure that your spending stays in balance with your income. If you need help with money management and setting up a realistic budget, look for low-cost classes or support from a local community college or government agency. Many local governments, credit unions and human services

agencies offer assistance to people wanting to learn basic financial planning skills. Take advantage of them as you develop your financial plan of action. If you recalculate your net worth every six months, you can chart your progress towards paying off your debts and reaching your financial goals.

If your net worth is positive, you'll still want to recalculate your net worth at least once a year to make sure that you're staying on the right financial path. Of course life events have a way of messing with our carefully made plans, so you might see your net worth drop from time to time. As long as you have an updated plan to get it back on track for future growth, you're still headed in the right direction even if your net worth is lower than it was in the past.

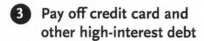

③ Pay off credit card and other high-interest debt

This may seem obvious, but remember that if you're paying your credit card company 17 percent interest on your balance every year, you could "earn" yourself a guaranteed 17 percent return by paying that balance off. So instead of putting extra money into a stock or mutual fund for an unknown return, use that money first to pay off all your credit card and other high interest debt. This applies to most car loans and department store charge balances, but not your mortgage or home equity loan because those usually carry a much lower interest rate.

Change your thinking about debt

Once you've reduced (or eliminated) your debt, make sure that you pay your new credit card balance in full every month so you can avoid interest charges entirely. If you're having a hard time making financial ends meet without carrying a credit card balance, concentrate your energy on resolving that situation before you commit any money to investments.

You can still learn as much as you can about investing in the meantime, but you're probably better served by making sure that your financial foundation is solid before you try to siphon

money away to invest instead of focusing on paying down high interest debt.

Do you really need to wait?

It may seem contradictory to hold off on investing until the financial basics are taken care of, but there's no sense squeezing your budget to find money to invest when you're better off reducing your debt first. Yes, investing is very important to your long-term financial future, but even more important is developing financial habits that will serve you well for a lifetime. Do you need to have the latest technological wonder in your home, and have it now? Or would you be willing to settle for something not quite as advanced but still functional, or scratch the purchase altogether, and put the money you save towards your future financial security?

We know we're asking you to put off or even give up some things you really want, but as a result of this sacrifice you'll achieve your financial goals more quickly. Only you can decide if the trade off is worth the effort. If you're not committed to your financial goals, then you're probably not going to be willing to make the difficult choices required to fulfill them.

The longer you carry high interest debt, the more money you're throwing at interest payments instead of into your investment account. Clear up your debt and avoid accumulating more by prioritizing your financial goals and living within your means to reach them. We won't pretend that paying off debt is easy. Help yourself by reaching out for support and taking advantage of whatever resources you can to teach you to live without relying on credit cards. (We list some of our favorite financial planning books at the end of this chapter). Once you're done making interest payments to your lenders, you can start applying that money towards your own financial dreams.

A few exceptions

Of course you're bound to find exceptions to every rule, though there's no guarantee every exception will be a good one. Here are three we think might be reasonable, but only after you've started a serious debt-repayment plan and are committed to not incurring additional debt. Retirement plans, investment clubs, dividend reinvestment plans (or DRIPs) and some mutual funds offer

individuals the opportunity to invest as little as $50 a month.

Retirement plans

If your employer offers a match on your retirement savings (for instance, they put in a certain amount of money for every dollar you contribute,) you may want to consider investing part of your income to take advantage of this "free" money, even if you're still in debt. It's never too early to invest towards your retirement, and establishing the habit as soon as you can is important. But debt-reduction is also important, so you'll have to decide how to balance the two.

Investment clubs

Investment clubs in particular can be a good option while you're paying off debt. You'll be learning about investing in an encouraging environment, and you'll be surrounding yourself with investors who will probably be most supportive of your attempts to become debt-free and learn to invest. Monthly contributions in some clubs can be as low as $10 or $25, offering an opportunity for you to start investing while still putting most of your money towards any high interest debt. We'll discuss investment club investing in greater depth in Part IV of this book.

Dividend reinvestment plans (DRIPs)

If you can't find a well-run investment club to join or aren't ready to start one of your own, dividend reinvestment plans (DRIPs) can allow you to make small monthly investments in individual stocks. Of course you'll need to learn the basics of stock analysis first so that you know you're investing in a quality company. You'll also need to watch out for DRIPs that charge commissions or monthly fees because these can quickly reduce your investment amounts. You can find a few Web sites with more DRIP information in the Online Resource Guide at the end of this book.

Stock mutual funds

A few mutual funds also offer the option of low investments if you commit to making the investment monthly. Again, you'll need to research the mutual fund and investigate management expenses and investment expenses.

You'll learn more about each of these options later in this book. These exceptions to the "don't invest until you pay down your debt" rule really should remain exceptions, though. We caution you against putting too much money into investments while you're still paying out a lot in interest. But if you're determined to invest regardless, at least do it on a small scale using one of these methods until you get your finances in better shape.

4 Set aside money for emergencies and planned expenses

As excited as you may be to start investing once your high-interest debt is reduced, we're asking you to slow down yet again. First you need to set aside a financial safety cushion to protect you against turning to credit cards or other debt in times of financial need. Many financial experts say you should have at least three to six months worth of living expenses set aside in an emergency savings account to protect against a rainy day.

One of the biggest reasons for this account is so that you won't have to go into debt to pay for unexpected expenses like car repairs, medical bills, or anything else that you wouldn't be able to pay off in time to avoid interest payments. You can also tap these savings to pay your rent or mortgage, food and utilities if you lose your job or can't work for some reason. This financial security blanket will allow you to sleep more soundly at night, and also help you practice the discipline you'll need to save money towards investing. We'll talk about where you should keep this emergency savings a little later.

Keep in mind the difference between saving and investing. Money you put in savings is money you may need quickly. You want to keep it accessible and you want to know that its value will stay roughly the same; this is money you can count on to be there in an emergency. Investing is something quite different.

When you invest, you're not only setting aside money, but you're taking measures for it to grow into more than you started with. You're investing to make a profit, but that can often take years. You shouldn't invest money that you may need immediate access to, only money that you don't anticipate needing for at least three to five years.

This is one reason why it's so important to have enough money in savings before you begin to invest. Investments vary in value from month to month, sometimes up and sometimes down. You don't want to be forced to sell your investments at a loss if you don't have enough money set aside in your savings account and you must dip into your investments during a temporary down time.

⑤ Purchase life and disability insurance

If you have a family or other people who depend on you financially, life insurance is very important. You can buy a solid, low-cost term life insurance policy from a reputable company to ensure that your dependents will be provided for in the event of your death. While any investments you own would certainly help, life insurance is most valuable to a beginning investor (unless you're so wealthy that your dependents would be fine without it).

People often disregard disability insurance, but it's equally important for financial security, whether you have dependents or not. If you're injured and unable to work, disability insurance can provide an essential income until you're healthy enough to bring in an income again. Disability insurance is especially important if you're single or can't depend on anyone else's income if you lose yours due to injury or illness.

There are many types of both life and disability insurance. Be sure to research the different policies before you purchase anything, and choose companies and policies with low expenses and preferably no commissions. *Term life insurance* is usually your best choice. It provides a straightforward insurance policy at the lowest premium because you're not buying protection or services you don't need (such as a cash value that you can access later under certain circumstances).

Above all, don't let anyone confuse you about combining insurance with investing. Insurance salespeople may highlight the benefit of cash value that comes with *whole life* or *universal life* insurance policies. But they're less likely to emphasize that these types of policies also carry hefty commissions and the premiums are much

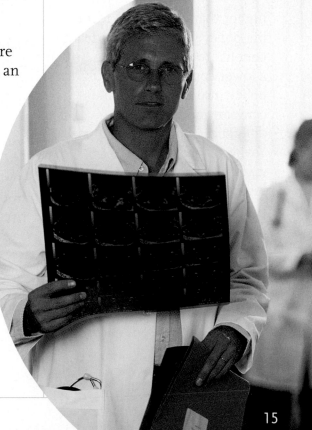

mend at the end of this chapter can help you learn what to look for (and what to avoid) when choosing insurance, as well as guidelines for how much insurance you should buy.

6 Investigate brokerage houses and mutual fund families

One of the keys to positive investment returns is keeping expenses low. Two mutual funds may perform equally as well, but if you buy the one with higher management expenses, your returns will be less. As you begin accumulating money to invest, start researching the financial firms you'll entrust that money to.

Many financial magazines and Web sites do annual brokerage surveys where they rate the brokers on a variety of criteria. These can be a good place to start looking for ideas. You can also refer to the brokerage scorecards at *www.Gomez.com* for opinions from actual investors (look in the *Consumers section* for the scorecards). After you've narrowed your choices a bit, do your own homework. (We'll give you some guidelines to use when researching a

brokerage firm or mutual fund family later in this book.) You can find additional resources for selecting a broker in the *NAIC Computerized Investing & the Internet Handbook*.

If you feel comfortable making your own investment decisions, you might choose a *discount brokerage* firm (as opposed to a full-service broker), where you'll find lower commissions and fees. With a full-service broker, you'll get advice on which stocks and mutual funds to buy, but you'll also pay much higher trading commissions in exchange for that information. NAIC can teach you to select your own stocks and mutual funds using proven techniques.

The same goes with mutual funds. There are quality, low-cost fund families where your investment money will go farther simply because you're paying less in management fees. Even if you're investing in mutual funds through a retirement plan and you don't have many fund families to choose from, you'll still want to analyze the few choices you do have. Part II of this book will guide you through some mutual fund analysis tools and help you learn what to look for in a mutual fund.

higher than those for a term life policy with the same death benefit. Your best bet is to buy a lower cost term life insurance policy through a reputable company and invest the difference in premiums yourself. Yes, your goal is to learn to invest, but not through a life insurance policy.

Don't let the differences between life insurance policies confuse you or tempt you to avoid dealing with the whole issue. Insurance is too important to your financial stability to ignore. The books we recom

7 Consider a consultation with a financial professional

If you're feeling overwhelmed by any of the six steps above, you may want to think about seeking professional guidance, at least on a limited basis. A financial professional can help you calculate your net worth, construct a debt-repayment strategy and analyze your investment needs. A financial professional can also help you decide how much you should be investing towards retirement, and how to combine that objective with paying down any debt you might have.

There is a small array of financial advisors available to help you. Here are some of the major categories of advisors:

- CFA – Chartered Financial Analyst – has taken a broad educational program from the Association for Investment Management and Research (AIMR). This professional designation requires about 750 hours of preparation, in addition to three major (day-long) examinations.

- CFP – Certified Financial Planner – has taken five college-level courses on personal financial planning, and passed an examination on each course. Sometimes accountants (CPAs) and attorneys are CFPs.

- ChFC – Chartered Financial Consultant – has passed exams on finance, investing, and insurance, in addition to having at least three years of experience in the financial industry.

- CLU – Chartered Life Underwriter – has been trained in life insurance and personal financial planning. Courses and exams cover such topics as: taxation, employee benefits, estate planning, investments, and insurance.

- Registered Representative (or stock broker) – has passed a test administered by NASD (National Association of Securities Dealers).

Looking for a financial professional

Remember, you don't necessarily need to use the services of a financial professional. Many, many successful investors chart their financial plan on their own. There's nothing wrong with a little handholding, though, especially as you get started. Even one session with a good advisor can help you prioritize your goals and devise a plan you can follow for years to come as you continue your financial education.

Choosing a financial advisor takes a little effort, though. Don't blindly hire the first person you find; do some research first. The most important factor in your choice should be how the person is compensated. Do they earn commissions or are they a *fee-only financial advisor?*

When "free" doesn't mean free

Some advisors may offer their services to you for free, and if you're working hard to pay down debt or save money towards investing, free financial planning might seem very attractive. You must realize, though, that you will end up paying in other ways if you take the advisor's investment advice.

Advisors that aren't fee-only accept commissions or other payments from the financial

services companies whose products they recommend. They may receive a large commission if you purchase a whole life insurance policy, or a payment from a mutual fund family whose funds they suggest you purchase. There's nothing unethical about this practice as long as the advisor is upfront about who compensates them and how, but not all advisors are forthcoming with this information unless you ask them directly.

Even if a potential advisor is very open with these details, you're still probably better off with a fee-only financial advisor. When a mutual fund or other financial services company is paying an advisor, you need to be concerned about possible conflicts of interest. It's not uncommon for such an advisor to recommend mutual funds with high management fees or even sales commissions simply because that fund company underwrites the "free" advice your advisor gives you by compensating the advisor in some way. Fee-only professionals don't have this conflict.

Pay your own way

Fee-only financial advisors are paid in only one way—by their clients. While it may seem more expensive to pay a planner upfront, you'll know that the planner is not biased towards any financial services, products or companies due to some type of financial arrangement with certain companies. If you specify that you want term life insurance and no-load mutual funds, your fee-only planner can help you decide what's best for your situation based solely on what's in your financial interest.

Finding a financial professional

Ask your friends and family for recommendations, and talk to at least two or three financial advisors before you make a final decision. You can use a financial advisor for a one-time-only consultation to get you started, or you may decide to consult with one every now and then to make sure you're still on track with your financial goals.

Be wary of any professional who pushes you towards investments you're not comfortable with or doesn't seem to listen to what you're saying. The advisor should be offering the guidance you need and are asking for, not pushing his or her own agenda.

Just remember that using a financial advisor isn't a requirement for becoming a successful investor. Trust yourself, reach out for help when you need it, and keep working towards developing the confidence to become a self-dependent investor. The more you learn, the less you'll need to rely on someone else's advice.

Questions to consider as you begin planning

1 Why do you want to learn to invest?

2 What are the most important financial goals you're working towards, and how many years do you have to reach them?

3 What will you need to do before you start putting aside money to invest? Do you have any high interest debt or other financial obligations to take care of first?

4 Do you have a savings account set up so you won't need to use credit cards to cover unexpected expenses? How much money should you keep in it?

5 Do you have the appropriate types and amounts of insurance to protect yourself and any dependents? If not, when will you start researching your options?

6 Have you asked friends or family for brokerage house or mutual fund family recommendations? Do you have a few prospects to start researching?

7 Will you need to consult with a financial professional, or would you rather get started on your own?

Now are you ready?

In this chapter, we've covered the importance of financial goal setting as well as the basics you should take care of before you even start investing. As you begin the process of becoming a successful investor, set some financial goals to work towards. Then plan a strategy to pay off any high interest debt you may carry and start funding an emergency savings account for short-term or unexpected needs. Investigate and purchase life and disability insurance if you don't already carry them. While you're taking care of all these pre-investing essentials, research brokerage houses and mutual fund companies so you can open accounts as soon as you're ready to start investing. Consult a financial profession-al if you think you'll need help creating a financial strategy.

A Few Good Books:

Since the focus of this book is on investing, we can't go into as much detail on personal finance as we'd like. If you need a little more information on the basics of financial planning and beginning investing, these books are a great place to start your research and find motivation for the journey ahead of you.

The Millionaire Next Door: Surprising Secrets of America's Wealthy by Thomas J. Stanley and William D. Danko, Pocket Books; 2000 (ISBN: 0743420373)

The Only Investment Guide You'll Ever Need by Andrew Tobias, Harvest Books, 2002 (ISBN: 0156011077)

Personal Finance for Dummies by Eric Tyson, John Wiley & Sons, 2000 (ISBN: 0764552317)

The Richest Man in Babylon by George S. Clason, Signet, 2002 (ISBN: 0451205367)

The Road to Wealth: A Comprehensive Guide to Your Money—Everything You Need to Know in Good and Bad Times by Suze Orman, Riverhead, 2001 (ISBN: 1573221813)

The Wealthy Barber: Everyone's Commonsense Guide to Becoming Financially Independent by David Chilton, Prima Publishing, 1997 (ISBN: 0761513116)

Why Invest?

Ready, Set...

Chapter 1 introduced you to the basics of financial planning, including what you should do before you start to invest. Now let's move on to why you should invest.

Savings vs. investing

You save money in the event of a rainy day; you want to be assured that the funds will be there when you need them, whether that's tomorrow or next year. You invest money that you won't need for a few years, with the expectation that it will grow over time. If you research your investments carefully and invest wisely over an extended period of time, investing is a proven and powerful way of increasing your wealth.

Investing can be much riskier than saving, though. Investors are willing to take on more risk in exchange for the possibility of greater financial rewards. Is investing worth the risk to you?

Risk vs. reward

Risk and reward go hand and hand. What all investors would like, of course, is a high reward or *return* with very low risk. Unfortunately, as investment risk goes down, so does the potential return. When you save money, you put it in a bank account somewhere where it will be safe. In exchange for this safety, you receive a small amount of interest on your money as your reward.

Investing your money instead of just saving it offers the potential for a much higher return. Not surprisingly, investing carries a greater risk than socking your money away in a bank savings account. If you seek a higher return by investing, you have to be willing to take on a higher risk that your investment may not perform the way you expect. The value of your investment might go up, but it also might go down. It might even go both up and down in value within a relatively short amount of time.

Watching out for volatility

This swing in value is called volatility, and *volatility* is the reason you shouldn't invest any money you'll need access to

within three to five years. If you've researched your investments carefully, you're hoping they'll grow in value over time. But you can't plan when the value of your investment will grow to be more than what you started with, or guarantee that it will grow at all. (There's that risk coming into play again).

Let's use the price chart of a fictional stock in Figure 2-01 to illustrate this point. Imagine you have $10,000 and you're trying to decide what to do with it. Should you put it into some sort of savings account or invest it instead? Your answer will depend on what you're planning to do with the money, and when.

Short vs. long-term investing

If you're planning to buy a house in two years, for instance, you wouldn't want to put the money for your down payment into an investment that falls in value right when it's time for you to write that big check. Investments like stocks and stock mutual funds are volatile; they rise and fall in value from month to month and year to year. Over the long term (five years or more in this case) the growth rate will smooth out. If you've chosen a successful investment, your $10,000 will have grown.

If you're forced to sell your investments after only two years because you need access

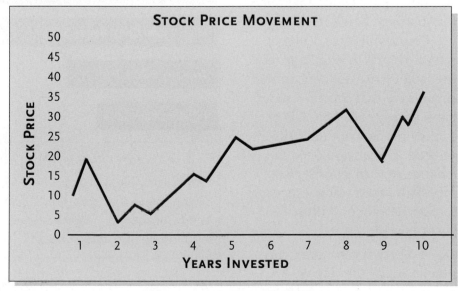

Figure 2-01: Price volatility

put your money whether you're saving or investing. In Chapter 3, we'll explain more about the relationship between risk and reward and your savings and investing options (as well as when—or when not—to use each type). For now, let's get back to the benefits of investing.

Why invest?

Investing is a wonderful way to increase your wealth. Living within your means so that you can save money for your future is very important. Over the long term, that money can grow faster than it would in a savings account if you invest it in shares of quality individual stocks or mutual funds.

Investing brings the deeper and lasting rewards of security and economic power that come from the accumulation of wealth.

When you invest, time is on your side. Stock and mutual fund prices are volatile, moving up and down in unpredictable swings. Wall Street goes through periods of growth—*bull markets*—as well as significant downturns—*bear markets*. But over the long haul, the stock market has always gone up, and patient stockholders can profit from that trend. In addition, investors who reinvest their earnings will see their money grow at an ever-increasing rate. ('We'll explain reinvestment later in this chapter).

As Figure 2-02 shows, the stock market has grown at an average

to that money, however, you'll not only miss out on the future growth, you'll end up with less money than you started out with. If you'll need your money in less than five years, you don't have much tolerance for volatility. You'll need to give up the possibility of a higher rate of return in exchange for the lower risk you'll encounter if you save that $10,000 in a bank savings account, CD or money market mutual fund instead. You always need to balance reward against risk, especially when you're expecting to use the money within a short period of time.

Don't worry if you're not sure how to make the risk vs. reward decision, or where to

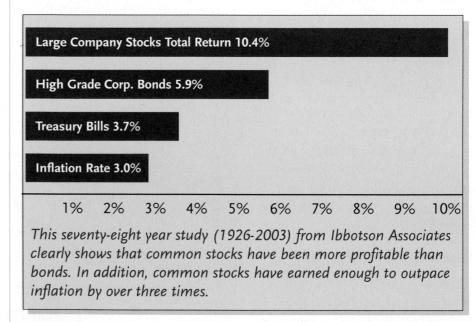

Large Company Stocks Total Return 10.4%

High Grade Corp. Bonds 5.9%

Treasury Bills 3.7%

Inflation Rate 3.0%

1% 2% 3% 4% 5% 6% 7% 8% 9% 10%

This seventy-eight year study (1926-2003) from Ibbotson Associates clearly shows that common stocks have been more profitable than bonds. In addition, common stocks have earned enough to outpace inflation by over three times.

Figure 2-02: Comparison of total returns of different types of investments

Rate of return	Years 5	Years 10	Years 20	Years 30	Years 40
3%	$19,442.50	$42,027.23	$98,736.83	$175,258.12	$278,512.39
5	20,486.83	46,778.79	123,823.89	250,717.91	459,713.57
8	22,190.01	55,249.70	177,884.17	450,088.55	1,054,284.37
10	23,424.71	61,965.61	229,709.07	683,797.60	1,913,034.07

Use this table to see how much you would save over a period of years at various rates of return if you invested $300 a month.

Figure 2-03: Building your portfolio

annual rate of 10.4% over the past 78 years. The bond market, by contrast, has returned 5.9%, and treasury bills have returned only 3.7% on average. NAIC suggests that your investment goal should be to double your investment portfolio every five years. You'll need to achieve an average 14.9 percent compounded annual growth rate to reach this goal. You won't see this rate of return every year. Some years your return may be much lower than the average and some it may be much higher. But by investing wisely, you should expect to achieve that average over the long term.

Even if your return is lower than 14.9 percent, your financial bottom line can still prosper if you're committed to investing over the long term.

Figure 2-03 shows how your portfolio can grow in value over various spans of time at different rates of return when you regularly invest $300 a month. An eight percent return is a conservative objective. If you invested $300 a month over twenty years at eight percent, your portfolio would be worth $177,884. Over thirty years, you would end up with $450,088.

To achieve consistent overall returns, you'll need to invest in quality stocks and mutual funds regularly, through both bull and bear markets. In this way, you'll invest when stocks are undervalued as well as when they're overvalued. This strategy of investing regularly regardless of how the stock market is valued is called *dollar cost averaging*.

Focus on the long term

When you first start investing, you may be nervous about timing. What if you make your first leap into stock ownership and the market takes a nosedive the next day? Are you doomed to lose everything? Time and experience will help you overcome this common fear. Market booms, recessions, depressions and recoveries are expected parts of the market cycle. Once you recognize the rhythm of these market phases, the volatility will no longer distract you. You'll even come to welcome market dips as an opportunity to invest more at bargain basement prices.

The magic of compounding

Investing over a long period of time is profitable in part because your earnings compound, and as a result grow by larger and larger amounts. *Compounding* is a simple idea. With compound interest, for example, you earn interest not only on your initial deposit, but on whatever previous interest your deposit has earned. If you deposit $100 in the bank and earn 6 percent, you'll have $106 at the end of the year. But if your account compounds annually, in the second year you'll earn 6 percent on $106, giving you $112.36 at the end of the year. At the end of 5 years, you'll have $133.82. The graph below shows the difference between investment totals when dividends are reinvested or paid out.

As you can see in the table, the gains created by compounding are modest in the early years; they really start to add up after two or three decades. At the bottom of the table, the numbers generated by each dollar grow at an impressive rate. The earlier you start investing, the greater the effect of compounding will be on your portfolio.

When you invest in the stock market, you make money in two basic ways—through the dividends which companies pay to their stockholders and by increases in the price of the

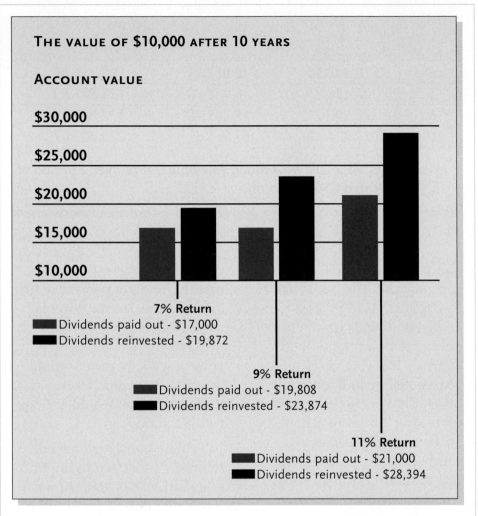

THE VALUE OF $10,000 AFTER 10 YEARS

ACCOUNT VALUE

7% Return
Dividends paid out - $17,000
Dividends reinvested - $19,872

9% Return
Dividends paid out - $19,808
Dividends reinvested - $23,874

11% Return
Dividends paid out - $21,000
Dividends reinvested - $28,394

Figure 2-04: Compounding growth combined dividend reinvestment

THE TABLE BELOW SHOWS WHAT AN ANNUAL INVESTMENT OF $1,000 INVESTED AT VARIOUS ANNUAL RATES OF RETURN MAY YIELD FOR AN AVERAGE INVESTOR.

Years Invested	4%	6%	8%	10%	12%
1	$1,040	$1,060	$1,080	$1,100	$1,120
5	5,600	6,000	6,300	6,700	7,100
10	12,500	14,000	15,600	17,500	19,700
15	20,800	24,700	29,300	35,000	41,800
20	31,000	39,000	49,400	63,000	80,700
25	43,300	58,200	79,000	108,200	149,300

Figure 2-05: Investing regularly over the long term

stock you own. When you reinvest the dividends, you're putting even more money to work through compounding.

Investing to beat inflation

Investing helps counteract the effects of inflation (the tendency for prices of the things you buy to rise over time). If your wages rise at about the same rate as prices, inflation won't bother you since you're not losing your buying power. Inflation does hurt, however, when you save or invest because the dollar you get back when you sell won't be worth as much as the dollar you invested.

If you put your money in a bank savings account, for example, and earn 1.5 percent interest but the inflation rate is 3 percent, you're losing money. Intelligent investing produces a higher return on your money than the rate of inflation. In spite of the bite inflation takes out of your money, you still come out ahead.

Other reasons to invest

In addition to the prospect of earning greater returns while beating inflation, you might reap other benefits from investing. When you invest in individual stocks and stock mutual funds, you become a partial owner of

a piece of corporate America. While you may only own a fraction of a company, you're still a shareholder, taking the same risks and hoping for the same rewards as the company itself. The money that shareholders invest when a company sells new shares enables that company to expand its operations, to buy facilities and equipment and to develop ideas into important products and services. If the company performs well and its stock price rises, you as a partial owner can claim your share of the gains.

Making it fun

There's another reason you might want to invest that you may not have considered. Investing is fun! The research involved in analyzing a stock or mutual fund can be as rewarding as any other hobby you might enjoy, and be profitable as well. You don't need a degree in accounting or business to learn what you need to know to make wise investing decisions.

As you develop your skills and start investing in profitable

growth companies, you might find yourself rooting for their success like a passionate sports fan. You'll start to not only make sense of financial publications, business news, and corporate annual reports, you might just find yourself enjoying them. As unbelievable as it might sound to any beginner, once you've invested your time and your money in those first few stocks, you'll probably find your enthusiasm for investing growing right along with your portfolio.

NAIC's Four Investing Principles

Now that you know why you should want to invest, it's time to turn back to the fundamental basis of NAIC's investment philosophy. These four principles have been leading investors to consistently superior returns since 1951.

1. Invest a set sum of money regularly over your lifetime

A beginning investor with limited funds can start investing with a little bit of that money every month, either on their own or through an investment club. A seasoned investor with more resources can build a solid financial future by investing regularly as well. Invest something in growth stocks and mutual funds every month and stay on track with your investment savings schedule. It doesn't matter how old or young you are now; investing is a lifetime project and you'll see the greatest results if you start right away.

2. Reinvest earnings, dividends and profits

Put everything you make back into your investments. If a company pays *dividends*, reinvest that money to buy more shares of either that stock or another. When you sell a stock, immediately put that money to work in another investment. Even if you start small, reinvesting dividends and earnings will help you build a substantial portfolio over time through the amazing effect of compounding we mentioned earlier in this chapter.

3. Buy growth stocks and stock mutual funds

NAIC suggests you set a goal of doubling your money every five years, which is possible by achieving an average 15 percent *compounded annual return* on your investments. How? By investing in growth stocks and growth stock mutual funds. Buy shares in businesses whose sales and earnings are growing faster than the overall general U.S. economy, and whose financial information suggests they'll be far more valuable five years in the future.

NAIC's investment tools will help you find profitable investments. Start by studying stocks and mutual funds you know and feel comfortable with, then branch out into new opportunities as you learn more.

Investment legend Peter Lynch, the highly successful former manager of Fidelity's Magellan mutual fund, recommends in his books that investors "buy what they know." This means looking at

Rate of return	Years				
	5	10	20	30	40
3%	$19,442.50	$42,027.23	$98,736.83	$175,258.12	$278,512.39
5	20,486.83	46,778.79	123,823.89	250,717.91	459,713.57
8	22,190.01	55,249.70	177,884.17	450,088.55	1,054,284.37
10	23,424.71	61,965.61	229,709.07	683,797.60	1,913,034.07

BUILDING YOUR NEST EGG

Use this table to see how much you would save over a period of years at various rates of return if you invested $300 a month.

Figure 2-06: Reinvesting dividends

the companies in your day-to-day life—retail stores, service businesses, banks in your community—for stock study prospects. Lynch talks about visiting his local shopping mall to see which stores were most crowded and then following up these leads with a thorough stock analysis before deciding whether or not to invest. You can do something similar when you're first looking for ideas of stocks to research. Who knows, you may find the perfect investment possibility right in your own backyard!

4. Diversify your investments

Since you can't guarantee which of your investments will be winners and which might not meet your expectations, you don't want to put all your money into just one investment. Along the same lines, don't risk everything on one type of stock or mutual fund. Invest in good companies of varying size and business sectors and in mutual funds from different categories or groups.

Diversification helps reduce risk and decreases your chances of "losing it all" by investing everything in a company or fund that performs much worse than expected. It's true that diversification can also limit your portfolio's upside potential, but diversification is important in order to balance risk and opportunity.

Don't diversify just for the sake of diversification, though. You're better served by a portfolio containing a small number of carefully chosen, quality growth companies than by one with a diversified yet inferior mix of many stocks.

Applying these four principles is not as hard as you might think. In the next chapter, we'll start discussing how to invest, and what you should invest in depending on your financial goals.

MOVING ON...

While saving is a vital habit to form, investing is even more important to your future financial success. Investing your money in appropriate places will help that money grow (both in value and through compounding). Over the long term, stocks and stock mutual funds offer higher returns than other investments and help counteract the effects of inflation.

NAIC's four investing principles give you a blueprint to follow as you begin your investing program. Investing regularly in a wide variety of companies, regardless of market activity will help you increase the odds of reaching your financial goals.

Risky Business

Introduction

Now that you've set your investing goals and taken care of your basic financial needs, it's finally time to start talking about investing. Here comes the fun part—learning about your investment options. How do you know whether you should put your money in stocks or bonds, money market funds or

real estate? It all depends on what your goals are and how long you have to reach them. What you invest in also depends on the level of risk you're willing to take. But first you need to learn what your investment alternatives are.

What's the risk?

Let's talk a little more about risk and its relationship with reward. Don't run away in horror; without risk, your chances of a decent investment reward are slim. When you understand how risk and reward work together, you're better prepared to choose appropriate investments.

In Chapter 2, we introduced the idea that the possibility of higher investment returns comes only when you're willing to take on higher risk. Investments with the lowest amount of risk, which are really more savings than investments, offer the lowest return. If you want a higher potential return, you need to be willing to accept more risk.

As we present the following descriptions of potential investment choices, we'll also discuss where each stands on the Risk Pyramid (see Figure 3-01). Follow along with this illustration, and you'll soon recognize the pattern of risk and reward.

Let's briefly run through some of your potential investment options now. There are a lot, but don't let the selections confuse or overwhelm you.

Once you start investing, your portfolio will most likely include only a handful of these. Don't expect exhaustive descriptions of these choices because you're not going to find that here. This section is only intended to

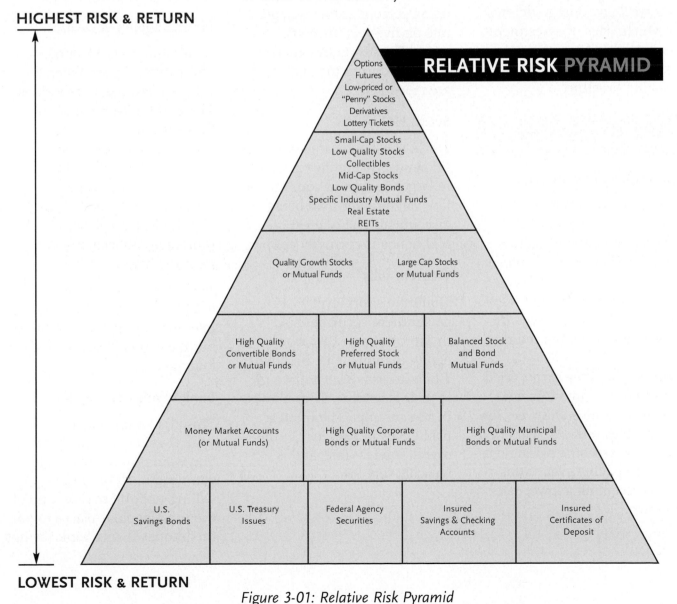

HIGHEST RISK & RETURN

RELATIVE RISK PYRAMID

Options
Futures
Low-priced or "Penny" Stocks
Derivatives
Lottery Tickets

Small-Cap Stocks
Low Quality Stocks
Collectibles
Mid-Cap Stocks
Low Quality Bonds
Specific Industry Mutual Funds
Real Estate
REITs

Quality Growth Stocks or Mutual Funds

Large Cap Stocks or Mutual Funds

High Quality Convertible Bonds or Mutual Funds

High Quality Preferred Stock or Mutual Funds

Balanced Stock and Bond Mutual Funds

Money Market Accounts (or Mutual Funds)

High Quality Corporate Bonds or Mutual Funds

High Quality Municipal Bonds or Mutual Funds

U.S. Savings Bonds

U.S. Treasury Issues

Federal Agency Securities

Insured Savings & Checking Accounts

Insured Certificates of Deposit

LOWEST RISK & RETURN

Figure 3-01: Relative Risk Pyramid

give you an overview of your possible choices. Use this chapter as a quick reference, and then do more research on the choices that appeal to you.

If you are interested in learning more about any of these types of investments that we don't discuss in the rest of the book, turn to the resources we suggest at the end of Chapter 1 for more information. Later in this book we'll give you guidelines for which types of investments are best suited for your portfolio, depending on your goals and investing timeline.

Level 1—
Lowest Risk/Lowest Return

Government investments

Savings instruments and securities issued by the U.S. Government are considered risk free. They are guaranteed by the federal government, which has the power to tax and create money. These types of investments are often referred to as *fixed income investments*, meaning that they earn a fixed rate of return. Investors who need investments with very low risk (such as retirees) will often choose fixed income investments for their stability even if this means accepting a lower rate of return.

Series EE bonds

These federal government savings bonds are issued in denominations as small as $50. A $50 savings bond is sold at a discounted rate of $25. By the time it reaches maturity, the interest earned plus the $25 purchase price will equal the $50 face value. The interest on a Series EE bond is a variable rate based on 85 percent of the average rate on five-year Treasury notes. The tax on the interest is deferred until the bonds are redeemed.

Series HH bonds

Series HH bonds are similar to EE bonds, except they are sold in larger denominations and at face value rather than being discounted. The interest on HH bonds is currently taxable.

Treasury bills

T-bills are short-term government securities sold in $10,000 to $1,000,000 denominations. Like EE bonds, T-bills are issued at a discount to their face value. They mature in 3-12 months. The interest paid varies in response to the overall interest rate, and is typically very low.

Treasury notes and Treasury bonds

These securities have longer maturities than T-bills. The notes mature in one to 10 years, the bonds in more than 10 years. Both are issued in minimum denominations of $1,000. Because of their longer maturities, Treasury notes and bonds normally pay higher interest rates than T-bills.

Federal agency securities

In addition to the federal government, many federal agencies issue debt securities. Three of the best known of these are the Government National Mortgage Association ("Ginnie Mae"), the Federal Home Loan Mortgage Corporation ("Freddie Mac") and the Federal National Mortgage Association ("Fannie Mae").

These federal agency securities tend to offer higher interest rates than the Treasury securities, but they are still considered low risk.

Bank savings accounts

Think of savings as the money you set aside for a rainy day. You want it to be there when you need it, so you're not willing to put it at risk. One of the most popular places to put this money is in a bank savings account. You won't make much in interest on the money in a savings account, but you will know that it's safe.

Bank savings accounts come with very little risk, especially since the Federal Deposit Insurance Company (FDIC) insures most commercial banks and savings and loan (S&L) savings accounts up to $100,000. Remember that in exchange for this low risk, though, you get very little reward.

Level 2—
Low Risk/Low Return

Money market accounts

When we mention *money market accounts*, we're not talking about the money market account your bank may offer (a sort of souped-up savings account that may pay out a little more in dividends than a savings account does in interest but also requires a much bigger minimum balance). These are money market mutual funds offered by mutual fund families and brokerage houses, and are usually composed of low-risk, relatively short-term securities such as Treasury bills, large CDs and notes issued by large, stable corporations. Money markets are considered safe places to park your short-term money.

Money market funds offer a perfect place to stash the

emergency savings we recommended in Chapter 1 that you should start accumulating. Many money market accounts offer free check writing or an ATM card you can use to access your money when you need it. Just be sure to find out if there's a minimum dollar amount before you write a check. Some money market funds won't allow checks for amounts less than $100 or $250, for example.

Since the account is for your emergency savings, though, you won't be writing small checks as you would in your personal checking account and a higher minimum most likely won't matter. Mutual fund companies set this higher minimum to keep their transaction costs lower, and the lower their expenses, the more they'll be able to pay out to you in dividends.

You should look for a money market fund offered by a reputable *mutual fund family or brokerage*, and especially one that charges low management fees and no load or *commission*. True money market funds are not risk free. Although they're

very safe compared to other places you might put your money, there is a slight risk you might lose some of your principal (the money you start out with). In exchange for this risk, you'll be rewarded with a higher dividend payout than the interest paid in a bank savings account.

Money market funds typically pay at least 1–2 percent more than bank savings or money market accounts, but with relatively little increased risk. The biggest drawback to using a money market fund for beginning investors is that the minimum balances can sometimes be more money

Pulling It All Together

Introduction

You invest hoping to end up with a return on your money that will allow you to meet your financial goals. But what exactly is your return, and what type of return can you reasonably expect from your investments? Your return will depend on the asset classes you choose for your portfolio, as well as the effect of factors such as taxes, expenses and inflation. Even after you've decided what types of assets to invest in, you'll need to determine how much of your investment money should go into each asset class to achieve the returns you're hoping for. Determining and following an appropriate asset allocation strategy is an important part of your investment planning. It's also important that you create an investment philosophy, the "big picture" guidelines you'll follow when you make investment decisions.

The importance of returns

You can't come up with a practical asset allocation plan, which we'll talk about a little later, unless you're realistic about your portfolio returns. Your return is the profit you make on an investment. If you invest $2000 in a stock, for example, and end up with $2200 after a year, your return would be 10 percent (the increase between what you invested and what your investment grew to, including any dividends paid during that time). $2200 (the final investment value) minus ($2000) the starting investment value) equals $200. This $200 gain (or profit) represents 10 percent of your $2000 initial investment.

Of course, as with many financial topics, calculating your return isn't quite that simple. Your return in this example is your nominal return. What you need to focus on is your real return. Keep in mind that investments do go down at times, so your

returns won't always be positive, but we'll stick to positive returns as our examples in this chapter.

Nominal vs. real returns

Your *nominal return* is the number you arrive at using simple arithmetic, just as we did in the example above. You start with a certain amount of money and end up with (you hope) a larger amount of money. You subtract the smaller number from the larger and that's your nominal return. But your nominal return isn't your *real return* on your investment. In order to find that real return, you'll need to consider three factors that can negatively affect your initial return.

1 Commission costs/expenses

Few things in life are free, and unfortunately investing isn't one of them. In order to buy and sell individual stocks, you'll usually need to pay a commission. Before you can calculate your real return, you'll need to add in the cost of doing business with a brokerage house. Using the numbers above, here's how the scenario might work. We'll use a hypothetical commission of $19.95 per trade, a typical commission if you're working with a discount broker online.

You'll pay $19.95 to buy the stock in the first place, then another $19.95 when you decide to sell. Altogether you've now paid $39.90 for the privilege of buying and selling your chosen stock, so you'll need to deduct that amount from your gain.

If you're purchasing mutual funds instead of individual stocks, you're still paying expenses but they're harder to identify. Most mutual fund expenses and fees are deducted from the fund's return. You wouldn't even notice them unless you went looking through the fund's financial reports. We'll cover mutual fund expenses and fees more thoroughly in Part II. You don't need to worry about them for the purposes of our discussion now.

2 Taxes

If you're lucky enough to see a positive return on your investments in taxable accounts, guess what? You'll be giving part of it to the IRS in the form of a tax on capital gains. While this may be frustrating, don't hold off on selling a stock you have a large gain in just because you'll have to pay taxes on your gain. If you have valid reasons for selling the stock (see Chapter 9 for more on selling), sell with the recognition that, even after taxes, you're still ending up with more than you started out with. Of course, there's no reason to pay more in taxes than you need to. Pay attention to short vs. long-term capital gain tax rates, and know the rules of each before you make selling decisions. Be aware of how a tax loss may affect your overall tax situation as well if you're faced with selling a losing rather than winning stock.

3 Inflation

Although inflation isn't often on the radar screen of many investors, it does have an impact on investment returns. There's nothing you can do to control inflation, but you should make allowances for it in your investment planning. Because inflation

many dollars. This swing in value is a sign of volatility.

Over the course of a year or many years, this price movement averages out to a steadier curve. When you watch prices in the short term the volatility can be frightening or exciting, depending on whether the movement is down or up. If you can't sleep at night for worrying about these swings, that's a good indication that you might want to adjust your asset allocation to include less stock and more fixed income investments.

Managing returns

Some financial experts say that proper asset allocation can account for up to 80 percent of your investment returns over the years, meaning that more important than which particular investments you choose are the percentages of stocks vs. bonds vs. cash you hold in your account. Their reasoning is that if you hold most of your money in stocks when stocks are performing well, or most of your money in cash when stocks are on a downturn, you'll end up ahead regardless of which individual stocks you're invested in.

The problem with this theory is that it's difficult for you as an investor to know when to switch your funds between asset classes to take advantage of these types of market changes. It's just as difficult for seasoned money managers to make the same decisions, so don't feel bad. There's just no proven way to accurately predict market movements well enough to ensure that your portfolio is primed for whatever the market is about to do next. Constantly rebalancing your portfolio means higher transaction costs, too, as you buy and sell according to what you think might happen in the market in the future.

A more reasoned approach to managing your investment returns through asset allocation is to research the average historical returns of each asset class before deciding what portion of your portfolio to put in each. You can rebalance the percentages once a year if necessary, and change your asset allocation model as your circumstances change.

What are the rules?

Unfortunately, there's no such thing as a standard, one size fits all asset allocation formula. Sure, there's the one that says, "Subtract your age from 100 and invest that percentage in stocks." Under this advice, a 55 year old would invest 45 percent of their available investment dollars into stocks. But not all 55 year olds are in the same place financially or have the same goals or risk tolerance.

Take two women, both the same age with the same $25,000 they've just received as an inheritance. The first woman retired early five years ago and doesn't plan to work any more, so her current investments will need to last her the rest of her lifetime. She may choose to be more conservative with her investments and invest a higher percentage into an income-generating bond fund instead of into stocks to provide for her current cash flow needs.

The second woman started investing for her retirement only a year or two ago and will

need to work many more years before she can accumulate enough investments to retire comfortably. She may choose to invest a much higher percentage in stocks than recommended by this simplistic formula, hoping to achieve the better rate of return that stocks have traditionally given compared to bonds.

Why is asset allocation important?

Many financial experts consider asset allocation to be key to your portfolio's performance. Books, academic studies and Web sites devoted to the topic abound. It's very easy to become confused or overwhelmed by often conflicting asset allocation advice. Ultimately, only you can decide what your ideal asset allocation is, and you should expect that it will change with time as your financial needs and goals change.

Generally, the younger you are and the more years you have to save for retirement, the higher your allocation of stocks and stock mutual funds will be. The closer you get to retirement, when asset preservation becomes more important than asset growth, the higher your allocation of bonds or other income-generating investments will most likely become.

Determining your asset allocations

In order to determine the most beneficial asset allocation for your current place in your investment timeline, you'll need to analyze your financial goals, your tolerance for risk and your available assets. We encouraged in Chapter 1 that a fee-only financial professional can help you figure out a financial plan when you're first starting out. A good financial professional can also help you establish your initial asset allocation plan as well as discuss how it may change over the years.

If you don't have a trusted financial professional or choose to make these decisions on your own, here are some questions to consider as you work to determine your asset allocation plan.

1 **Which asset classes will you be putting your investment money into?**

As explained earlier, the most common choices for investors are:

- U.S. stocks/stock mutual funds

- International stocks/stock mutual funds

- Fixed income (primarily bonds, bond mutual funds and fixed-income deferred annuities)

- Investment real estate (rental properties, REITs, limited partnerships)

- Cash (primarily money market funds, CDs—which can also be considered "fixed income" if the term is more than a year—and Treasury bills)

2 **What is your risk tolerance?**

Do you have many more years of employment ahead of you, potentially enabling you to take more risk by investing more heavily in stocks? Or are you currently retired and wanting to reduce your investment risk by investing primarily in income-generating asset classes? These questions, and more, need to be considered but there's no "one size fits all" answer. The *NAIC Using Portfolio Management Wisdom Handbook* can give you more guidance as you determine your tolerance for risk.

3 **How long is your investment horizon?**

Is this money you'll be investing for longer than five years, making it more suitable for stocks? Or will you need it in six months or a year, thus making cash a more appropriate choice?

4 **What are your goals for these investment dollars?**

If you're investing for retirement in thirty years, you'll probably want to put more of your investment dollars into stocks, which have a higher historical average rate of return. (Refer to Figure 2-02 in Chapter 2 if you need a visual reminder). But if you're thinking of investing money you'll need for a down payment in three years, you'll want to choose someplace less volatile than the stock market to put your money. The longer you have for your money to work for you, the more aggressive you might choose to be with your investment choices.

Calculating your current asset allocation

Once you have a clear understanding of your answers to these questions, you should calculate what your current asset allocation is. Add up your total investments, and then separate them into the five loose categories above (U.S. stocks, international stocks, fixed income, real estate and cash). Calculate the percentage you currently own in each category, then match those categories up with a general return you might use to estimate

potential returns. (See Chapter 2 for some historical returns you might want to use when making estimates). Using these percentages and your estimates for future returns, are you on track to meet your financial goals? As mentioned earlier, a fee-only financial professional can be instrumental in this process if you find that you want more personalized guidance.

Asset allocation vs. diversification

Don't confuse asset allocation with diversification. Although related, they are not the same. Both try to manage your investment returns by managing risk, but while diversification keeps you from investing too much of your money into one particular investment (such as your employer's stock or one single technology mutual fund), asset allocation spreads your investment dollars across distinctive asset classes in an attempt to achieve the highest returns you can while preserving the money you need to keep safe.

Put another way, diversification spreads your stock and mutual funds across a variety of industries and market caps (large, medium and small) to reduce the risks that come from investing everything in one particular type of stock or mutual fund. Asset allocation offers a way to reduce risk or

improve returns by balancing your total portfolio of investments across different asset classes—a certain percentage in stock vs. fixed income vs. cash investments depending on your financial goals and timeline. You can learn more about asset allocation and portfolio management in general in the *NAIC Using Portfolio Management Wisdom Handbook*.

Bringing it all together

Beyond NAIC's four investment principles that we introduced previously—invest regularly over the long term, reinvest all earnings, invest in quality growth companies, and diversify your portfolio—here are some other sound investment guidelines to follow regardless of what type of investments you choose:

1 **Define your investment philosophy**

Your investment philosophy is your financial mission statement. Before you start investing, you'll want to have a loose set of rules to guide you. If you agree with NAIC's basic investment philosophy, your personal investment philosophy would mirror it closely.

Whatever guidelines you decide to follow, write them down and keep them in mind as you make investment choices over the years. Adjust it to keep it relevant to your circumstances. Above all, try to follow it as closely as you can to ensure that you stay on the investment path geared towards helping you achieve your financial goals as quickly as possible and with the least amount of risk.

Here's one example of an investment philosophy. Think a little about your own goals and investment beliefs after you read it. Then take a few minutes to draft your personal investment philosophy.

2 Stick to one strategy

If your investment philosophy says that you want to follow a long-term buy-and-hold strategy, selling only for well-defined reasons (which we'll cover briefly in Chapter 9), follow it. Don't decide one day to start day trading or buying speculative stocks because you think that's the way to goose your portfolio's return. If you really do believe this (and here's hoping you don't), then you've undergone a fundamental shift in your investment philosophy and it's time to revamp your entire strategy.

Pick an investment strategy you're comfortable with, one that will help you achieve your financial goals, then stick to it closely as you make your investment decisions. Do whatever research you've decided is necessary, choosing investments that meet your pre-defined criteria. You'll find that following a set investment strategy frees you from even considering inappropriate investments, saving you time and potentially money.

If you're really itching to experiment outside of your usual investment strategy but you're afraid you'll make costly mistakes with

SAMPLE INVESTMENT PHILOSOPHY

My investment objective is to build a diversified portfolio that includes quality growth stocks and mutual funds, balanced according to my personal asset allocation model and focused on achieving my financial goals. I'll create this portfolio based on the results of my detailed research, focusing on investments I intend to hold for the long term.

MY INVESTMENT PHILOSOPHY

_____

_____

_____

_____

_____

your portfolio, consider an additional option. Some investors allocate a small part of their portfolio, maybe five percent or less, as "mad money," money they've decided in advance they'll take more risks with. If you have enough resources to feel comfortable risking the money, then incorporate this idea into your overall investment plan.

Just be sure to acknowledge that while it's possible to hit the jackpot by investing in penny stocks or something else equally risky, you're more likely to watch these speculative investments go to zero. Investing only a tiny percentage of your portfolio helps you work through your speculative urges in a way that won't break your personal bank, allowing you to stay focused on a more reasonable plan for the bulk of your investing dollars.

❸ Keep expenses low

If you're investing in mutual funds, look for *no load* funds as opposed to funds that carry loads or sales charges. *Index* mutual funds typically charge much lower management fees than actively managed funds. We'll explain these different types of funds in more detail in Part II. The bottom line, though, is that you can often increase your mutual fund returns by choosing funds with low management expenses, no sales charges and low portfolio turnover.

If you're investing in individual stocks, search out brokerage firms with low commissions and fees. Whenever possible, you'll want to keep your investment expenses below 2 percent, and preferably no higher then 1 percent, of the amount you'll be investing. This means that if your brokerage charges $19.95 to buy a stock, you should be purchasing at least $1995 worth of stock to keep your commission expenses at one percent. You'll be paying the same commission to sell the stock, of course, doubling your commission expense. If you've chosen a quality stock and hold it for the long term though, the value of the stock should increase, decreasing the commission percentage overall.

Research your many options for buying and selling stock, including online discount brokerages, dividend reinvestment plans (DRIPs), NAIC Low Cost Plan, and companies such as ShareBuilder that allow small purchases for minimal commissions. You'll find more information about choosing a brokerage and keeping your expenses as low as possible in Chapter 9.

❹ Do your own research

Don't trust anyone else's opinions about the investments you're considering for your portfolio, at least not until you do your own research. Brokerage and media analysts can sometimes have conflicts of interest you don't know about that might affect their opinions. You can be sure that they don't know the peculiarities of your own portfolio or your investment goals—only you know what types of investments will suit your purposes best.

You'll find plenty of guidance for researching your own investments throughout this book. It's not as hard as you might think to learn what you need to know to make well-informed, reasonable choices for your personal portfolio. Don't trust hot stock tips from some expert you see on TV (or your next door neighbor) until you do your own homework. If you find that it really is a hot stock tip, then act on it with the clear understanding of where you're investing your money. In the greater likelihood that you find the tip a bust, move on with the knowledge that by doing your own research, you've protected yourself from a shoddy investment.

5 Hold for the long term

When you do finally invest in stocks and mutual funds after researching them thoroughly, confirming that they fit your investment philosophy and that you've kept your expenses as low as possible, you've most likely chosen high quality investments with great prospects for future growth. Hold on to them. Don't sell after a few years just because the price hasn't changed much.

If the basic reason for choosing the investment hasn't changed (the earnings are still solid, for example), be patient. No one ever said long-term investing would be exciting.

Sometimes you'll need to wait a few years for your investments to start to pay off. If you sell too soon, you'll miss your chance at better returns.

That's not to say you should never sell. If the reasons you bought the stock or mutual fund do change, then it may very well be time to take your gains (or cut your losses) and move on to an investment with a brighter outlook. No matter how good your research is, there will always be corporate developments you could never predict.

NAIC's *Rule of Five* is a "rule of thumb" statement about portfolio expectations, based on general observations. It says that of every five stocks owned over a five-year period, one will outperform your expectations, three should perform about as well as you expected, and one will fall below your expectations. In Chapter 9, we'll briefly cover how to determine if one of your investments is in fact an underperformer, as well as valid reasons for selling investments even when you have a long-term investment philosophy.

MOVING ON...

When you're contemplating potential returns for your portfolio, don't forget to take into account how investment expenses, taxes and inflation might reduce your real returns. It's better to slightly underestimate the return you think you'll get when you're planning than to think your investments will earn the highest return possible. Wouldn't you rather be pleasantly surprised when your portfolio returns more than you'd planned for, instead of caught in a shortfall because you were overly optimistic?

Appropriate asset allocation can make a noticeable difference in your portfolio's returns. Determining what your best allocations are isn't always simple, though. Take another look at the financial goals you identified earlier in the book to identify your investment timeframe, then choose a mix of investments most likely to meet those goals in the time you have.

Tax-Advantaged Investing

Introduction

While your investment philosophy will remain the same whether you're investing in a taxable or tax-advantaged account, your investment alternatives might not be the same.

Before you begin investing, you should decide on an allocation strategy to determine what percentage

you'll be investing in retirement or college savings accounts and what percentage in taxable accounts. This chapter will explain the basics of the most popular tax-advantaged investment choices as well as some differences you should keep in mind.

Investing in tax-advantaged and other retirement accounts

If you're working, you most likely have access to some type of retirement investment option, whether through your employer's plan or through an IRA you invest in on your own. Investing for your retired years should be one of your top investment priorities. If you have any choice of investment vehicles (deciding which mutual funds your retirement money will buy, for example), this is the perfect place to start putting your new investment knowledge to work. Chances are that you have to make some sort of choice about how your retirement money is invested, so it's in your best interest to learn how to analyze your choices instead of blindly choosing based on a fund's name or what your co-workers invest in.

One reasonable investment policy is to contribute the maximum to your tax-deferred investment alternatives before investing retirement or college savings in taxable accounts. You'll most likely want to invest in taxable accounts for other important financial goals, such as saving for a house, car or other long-term goals. If you've maxed out your tax-deferred retirement and college accounts and still have savings to invest, congratulations! You have plenty of choices, including brokerage and mutual fund accounts. We'll tackle these subjects in later chapters, so let's finish with tax-deferred accounts first.

We're only offering a general overview of some of the tax-deferred options you might have available to you. Before making choices about which accounts are best for you or investing any money into them, please do more research on your own or talk to a tax professional. The list of personal finance books at the end of Chapter 1 is a great place to start a deeper investigation. The IRS's Web site *(www.irs.gov)* is another valuable source of information.

Pre-tax retirement accounts

Many retirement plans are funded through pre-tax contributions. This means that your taxable income is reduced by the amount that you contribute to your 401(k) or traditional (as opposed to Roth) IRA account, for example. If you contribute $3000 to a traditional IRA for a specific year, you do not pay taxes on that amount of income. When you withdraw money from a tax-deferred account, most likely at retirement (otherwise you'll usually pay a penalty), both the contributions and any earnings will be taxed at your regular income tax rate.

By deferring these income tax payments until you withdraw the money from your account, you receive even greater returns through the "magic" of compounding that we explained in Chapter 2. The more money you contribute, the more opportunity for those contributions to build on themselves, and the greater chance for your account to grow larger over the years. This chart illustrates the benefits of investing long term in a tax-deferred over a taxable account.

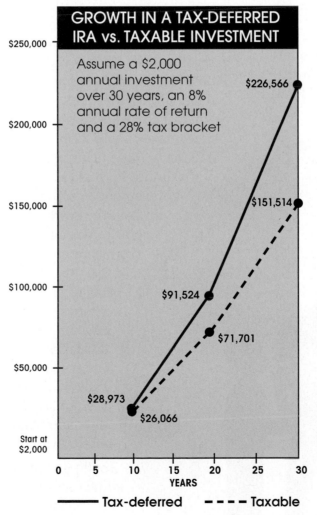

GROWTH IN A TAX-DEFERRED IRA vs. TAXABLE INVESTMENT

Assume a $2,000 annual investment over 30 years, an 8% annual rate of return and a 28% tax bracket

$250,000
$200,000
$150,000
$100,000
$50,000
Start at $2,000

$226,566
$151,514
$91,524
$71,701
$28,973
$26,066

YEARS
0 5 10 15 20 25 30

—— Tax-deferred   – – – Taxable

Figure 5-01: Tax-deferred vs. taxable

Employee Retirement Plans

Employer-funded *defined benefit* pension plans are becoming increasingly rare for employees outside the government and education spheres. Defined benefit plans guarantee employees a certain percentage of their salary when they retire, depending on current salary and years of employment. The employer chooses how the money is invested, and the employee has practically no control over the process other than to cash the benefit check when it arrives.

Most employers now offer *defined contribution* plans, usually through 401(k)s, which we explain in more detail below. In this type of employer retirement plan, the employer may contribute a "defined" amount of money to an employee's account, which is controlled by the employee. Also, the employee may contribute dollars to his own account.

Defined contribution plans

401(k) and 403(b) plans are both examples of employer-sponsored tax-deferred retirement plans. A 403(b) plan is similar to a 401(k) plan except that 403(b)s are for employees of nonprofit organizations such as schools, hospitals, foundations and religious organizations. You can contribute a certain percentage of your earned income to these plans, up to a maximum limit set by the government. You can find out the current contribution limit from your employer or the IRS. These plans offer a significant tax advantage since dividends, interest and capital gains are not taxed until you make withdrawals.

403(b) qualified employees are often provided with other deferred compensation vehicles for retirement income, usually in the form of annuities. Check with your employment benefits office to determine which retirement investment alternatives are available to you.

Check with the IRS for the current age at which withdrawals may begin—there can be expensive penalties for withdrawals before you reach this age. You may, however, be allowed to make a penalty-free withdrawal from some plans for college tuition or medical emergencies. Your employer or the IRS can give you more specific details about these options.

Some employers match part of each employee's contributions. If your employer offers a fifty percent match, that means for every $100 you contribute, your employer will contribute another $50. If you're lucky enough to have an employer match in your 401(k) or 403(b), make it a priority to contribute at least up to the maximum that your employer will match. This "free" money will probably be the fastest, most risk-free return on an investment you're ever likely to earn.

Your 401(k) and 403(b) contributions are automatically withheld from your paycheck on a pre-tax basis, meaning

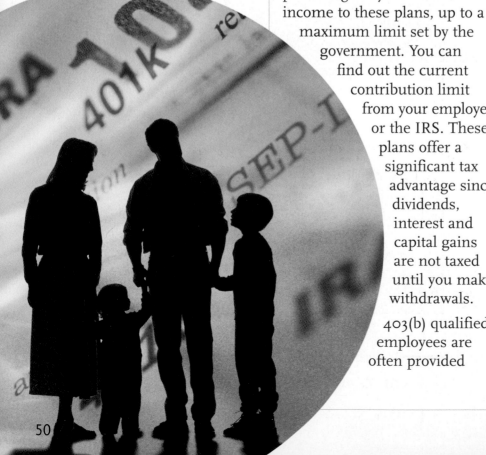

that you don't pay income tax on the amount you're contributing, at least until you withdraw it after you've retired. Your contributions are deposited into the professionally managed investment account that you've designated. You typically have a choice of mutual funds to invest your contributions in, usually stock growth funds, a balanced fund (stocks and bonds), a bond fund and a money market fund. There may be both index and managed mutual funds to choose from (more on the differences between them in Chapter 10).

Individual Retirement Accounts (IRAs) and other plans

If you're self-employed or not covered by an employer-sponsored retirement plan, you can still save for your retirement in a tax-advantaged account by investing through an Individual Retirement Account (IRA). *Traditional IRAs* allow you to save on a pre-tax basis—any contributions you make are deductible when you file your taxes. Your withdrawals at retirement are taxed at your income tax rate. *Roth IRAs* allow you to invest on a tax-free basis as well, but you contribute after-tax dollars. This means that your withdrawals at retirement won't be taxed at all.

Traditional IRAs

If you're not covered by an employer-sponsored retirement but you do have earned income, you can contribute to a tax-deductible traditional IRA. You can also make contributions for a non-employed spouse. The annual contribution limit varies depending on your age and income. You can contribute to a traditional IRA even if you are covered under an employer-sponsored investment plan, but your contributions will not be tax-deductible.

As with all the other retirement plans, check with the IRS or your tax professional for complete details, including current contribution limits and any income restrictions. For traditional IRAs, the income tax deduction is phased out after you reach a certain income level, and you may not contribute more than your earned income. Even if your contributions aren't deductible, your capital gains and dividends will still grow tax-deferred until they are withdrawn.

Plans for the self-employed/business owner

If your employer is you, don't worry; you still have plenty of options for investing towards your retirement. Talk to your tax professional about whether or not you qualify for/should contribute to a SEP-IRA, SIMPLE IRA or Keogh Plan. Each plan has different requirements and different advantages, so you'll want to research carefully before making a choice.

Roth (after-tax) IRAs

Technically, Roth IRAs are tax free. Contributions to a Roth IRA are made with money that's already been taxed. No further tax is collected on either your original contributions or on any earnings or capital gains they produce. You can even withdraw your original contributions without penalty after a certain number of years (check the IRS Web site at *www.irs.gov* for the most updated Roth IRA regulations).

If you currently have a traditional IRA account, you can convert it to a Roth IRA. You'll have to pay taxes on the converted amount. An IRA conversion may or may not make financial sense depending on your age and other factors, so it's worth talking to your tax professional about if you're considering it.

Other tax-advantaged investment alternatives

Besides retirement accounts, you have other options for investing in tax-deferred accounts. Although this may sound repetitive, be sure to check with the IRS or your tax professional for guidance on any contribution or income limits for these choices.

Tax-Deferred Annuity (TDA) insurance contracts

If you've maxed out your employer-based retirement accounts and IRAs, you do have another option for tax-deferred retirement investing—annuities. An *annuity* is a type of investment contract used to provide

future income. While traditionally offered by insurance companies, you can now purchase annuities from other providers as well.

Because annuity earnings are tax-deferred until distribution, they're useful once you've exhausted all your other retirement savings options. When you purchase an annuity, you contract with an annuity issuer to pay in contributions and the insurance company agrees to pay out a certain amount of income distributions over a certain number of years, usually far in the future. These are paid to the beneficiary, which may be you or someone you choose (a spouse or child, for example).

Annuities can charge relatively high management expenses, and there can also be substantial fees (called surrender charges) if you attempt to cash out early. Also, you must use after-tax dollars to fund an annuity, so your contributions are not tax-deductible. If you do decide that an annuity is right for your situation, be sure to compare choices from a few different companies. Management expenses, other fees and

investment options can vary greatly and will affect the return on your investment. You'll also want to completely research the tax treatment of annuity distributions so you won't run into any surprises down the road.

College savings plans

Thanks to relatively new college savings plans, parents, grandparents and others can now reap tax benefits while saving for their favorite child's higher education needs. One of the accounts can even be used for qualified educational expenses for elementary, middle and high school students. Check the Online Resource Guide in Appendix A for Web sites to help with college savings plan research.

Section 529 plans

Section 529 plans are offered by almost every state, with a variety of different contribution limits and investment options. Withdrawals are free from federal income tax if used for qualifying college expenses, and contributions to 529 plans are even tax-deductible in some circumstances. If the family member you set up the plan for doesn't use up all the money in the account, funds can be transferred to another family member without tax penalty. Since investors are not limited to their own state's plan, you should research your options carefully before choosing the best one for your particular circumstances.

Section 529 plans do have some downsides you'll want to investigate. Each state sets its own investment options, maximum account contribution, management expenses and tax benefits, leading to a confusing array of choices for investors trying to compare their options. Even if your state's plan is one with increasing annual management expenses, check to make sure you won't be missing out on a state income tax deduction or state tax-free withdrawals before choosing a different state's plan. The Online Resource Guide near the end of this book lists specific sites to visit if you're trying to research and choose between different state plans.

Coverdell Education Savings Accounts (ESAs)

Formerly called Education IRAs, *Coverdell Education Savings Accounts* (ESAs) are unique among college saving options in that tax-free withdrawals may be made for elementary and high school as well as college educational expenses. Parents may use ESA funds to pay for private school tuition and uniforms and educational computer

equipment, among other expenses. With higher annual contribution limits than in the past and more flexible investment options (as well as often lower management expenses) than Section 529 plans, ESAs have become an attractive savings vehicle for families within the eligible income range.

While ESA contributions are not tax-deductible, withdrawals for qualified educational expenses are tax-free. Any

money left in an ESA when the student beneficiary turns 30 is subject to tax and penalties, although unused funds can be transferred to another qualified family member under some circumstances. If your state's Section 529 plan doesn't offer any extra state tax benefits or charges high management fees (it may take a little research to track these down), ESAs could offer more of an advantage as long as you're within the income requirements.

MOVING ON...

Once you've utilized your tax-deferred and other retirement options, you'll probably want to consider investing in taxable accounts as well. If you're saving for a house, your child's education or another non-retirement financial goal, you'll most likely need to invest outside of your retirement account. Whether you open a brokerage account so you can buy individual stocks or buy shares of a mutual fund directly from the fund family, Parts II and III will help you learn to select quality investments to meet your goals.

Your investment portfolio should include both tax-deferred, tax free, and taxable accounts. The percentages will vary depending on where you are in your investment timeline, but you should be sure to make good use of tax-advantaged investment options such as your employer's retirement plan or your own IRAs. Tax-advantaged college savings options can also help you increase your higher education savings.

If you've maxed out your retirement plans or are investing for shorter term goals such as a house down payment, you'll be using taxable accounts in addition to your tax-deferred options. If you are investing in taxable accounts, be sure to keep tax ramifications in mind when you're choosing your investments or making selling decisions.

PART TWO:
Investing in Stocks

Stock Market Basics

Introduction

Now that you've got the basics of money management down, it's time to jump straight into the world of investing. We'll focus on the stock market in general in this chapter, then move on to analyzing and buying individual stocks in later chapters after we've explored these fundamentals.

What is a stock, and a stock market?

When you buy stock in a certain company, what you're purchasing is an actual piece of ownership in that company. Granted, it may be a very tiny piece and you won't have much say in how the company is run beyond annual shareholder votes, but you're still considered a partial owner even if you only own one share.

Private vs. public companies

You can't buy stock in just any company you're interested in because not every company is publicly traded. Privately held companies don't offer shares to the general public, and they're not required to disclose financial details such as their earnings and revenues.

Shares of publicly traded companies, on the other hand, are generally available through one of the stock exchanges to anyone interested in purchasing them. Publicly traded companies are also required by the Securities and Exchange Commission (SEC) to regularly report their finances according to established standards. This financial reporting is what provides investors with the information they need to research and analyze a company before deciding whether or not to purchase shares.

IPOs

When a privately held company decides to become publicly traded and offer shares on the open stock market, this process is called an *initial public offering* (IPO). While you've probably heard plenty of stories of people

making huge profits by investing in IPOs, there are many reasons to steer clear of them at least until you've had a few years of investing experience behind you.

Even then, investing in IPOs can be tricky. You may not have access to at least five years of financial information, making it difficult to properly research the fundamentals. Also, investors rarely have an opportunity to buy shares of the most promising IPOs. These are often informally reserved for the very best customers of the brokerage firms handling the offering.

These first investors frequently "flip" their shares, meaning they resell them almost immediately to capture their gains if the share price leaps up dramatically in the first hours or days after the IPO.

Investors who buy shares of these stocks on the secondary market (meaning when shares are exchanged between investors after they've gone on the public market) can end up paying inflated prices, only to watch their investment shrink in value after the IPO's stock price retreats to more reasonable levels.

Preferred vs. common stock

You may come across the term preferred stock at some point and wonder how it differs from common stock. Preferred stock resembles a bond more than a stock, and preferred stock holders enjoy a little more safety in some ways than common stock holders do. Preferred stock dividends, for example, are paid out before common stock dividends.

Also, if a company were to go bankrupt, preferred stock holders are given precedence over common stock holders when it comes to recovering any money. One drawback to preferred stock is that preferred stockholders generally have no say in how the company is run whereas common stock holders are eligible to vote in person or by proxy at the annual shareholder meetings.

When we discuss investing in stock throughout this book, we're referring to common, not preferred, stock. Preferred stockholders have priority for dividends and claims on assets, but common stock share prices are where the real action is, especially for growth companies. Preferred stock doesn't offer the same potential for growth as common stock, and is much more suitable for investors looking for income rather than growth in their portfolio.

The stock markets

There are two kinds of stock markets—exchanges and the over-the-counter (OTC) market. Exchanges such as the New York Stock Exchange (NYSE) and the American Stock Exchange (AMEX) are auction markets where buyers and sellers come together to do business. The NYSE, sometimes called "the big board," is the most well known and prestigious of the stock exchanges.

The over-the-counter or NASDAQ (National Association of Securities Dealers Automated Quotes) market is a dealer marketplace where securities dealers buy or sell from their own accounts. As a rule, smaller and newer firms as well as a number of technology companies are traded on the NASDAQ.

Why invest in stocks?

You should know by now that NAIC emphasizes investing in stocks (and stock mutual funds) as opposed to bonds or other investment alternatives, when investing for the long term. But do you know any of the reasons behind this belief?

Highest growth potential

We discussed the relationship between risk and reward in Chapter 3, and earlier you saw statistics showing that over time, stocks have rewarded investors with higher returns than bonds and cash investments. This fact is one of the major reasons that NAIC favors investing in stocks over the long haul. Stocks (and stock mutual funds) offer you a more attractive combination of risk and reward than other investments such as bonds and cash.

It may take a little time and commitment on your part to learn to analyze stocks, but the potential return on this investment of effort can be rewarding over the decades.

Tax efficiency

When you buy individual stocks (as opposed to stock mutual funds), you have much greater control over taxable events in your portfolio. Due to mutual fund distribution regulations, you may find yourself paying capital gains taxes every year whether or not you sold fund shares, even in years when the fund has a negative return. This can make tax planning difficult.

On the other hand, when you invest directly in individual stocks, *you* decide when you're going to buy or sell, and *you* decide if you want to incur capital gains by selling a stock in which you hold a gain. The same goes with tax losses. If you have a larger than average income or capital gain to pay taxes on and you also hold some losers in your portfolio, you can decide if you're going to hold those stocks or sell them and take a tax loss to offset your gains. When you invest in mutual funds, you give up part of your ability to make decisions like this.

Individual stocks can also be a more tax-efficient way to invest outside of retirement accounts. You can hold an individual stock for decades and not pay a penny in capital gains tax even if the stock price grows tremendously in value. You

have the power to defer paying taxes on those gains until you decide to sell. (Of course, you'll still owe taxes every year on any dividends the company pays out.) You can learn more about this and other aspects of portfolio management in the *NAIC Using Portfolio Management Wisdom Handbook*.

Stock market terminology

Navigating the stock market can sometimes be intimidating for beginners. The rest of this chapter covers some terms and concepts you'll probably encounter before too long.

Dividends

Some companies choose to pay out part of the corporate earnings to shareholders quarterly or annually in the form of *dividends*. You can reinvest these dividends in shares of the company if you participate in their Dividend Reinvestment Plan (DRIP) or through a brokerage that offers reinvesting, or you can choose to receive the dividends in cash.

Not every company pays dividends. Some choose to reinvest their earnings right back into the company in order to finance the company's continued growth. A company may decide to pay dividends after it has become more established. Once a company begins paying dividends, it rarely stops or reduces the dividend amount, as that would be an indication of shaky corporate finances. If indeed a company finds itself in financial difficulty, management may decide to suspend the dividend for a period or end it altogether in an attempt to rescue the company from failure.

Stock splits

If a company's share price moves higher and higher (past $100 is a common measure), management may decide to declare a stock split as a way to bring that share price down to a level deemed more popular by investors. In a two-for-one stock split, for example, shareholders end up with a total of two shares for every one share they owned at the time of the split.

These extra shares don't appear out of thin air, of course. When the stock splits, the share price splits as well. So if you owned one share of a $20 stock before the split, you would own two shares of a $10 stock after a two-for-one split. It's fun to think that your investment has been doubled, but nothing has really changed. Think of it as a pizza cut into eight slices instead of four. You may have twice as many slices, but they're only half the size of the original slices. The size of the pizza doesn't change, just the number of slices it's divided into.

Stock splits used to be more meaningful to investors in the days when brokerages would charge far higher commissions for stock purchases of less than 100 shares (an "odd lot"). If a company's share price grew too high, purchasing 100 shares (a "round lot") could prove financially out of reach for many investors. Stock splits helped keep shares of companies with rapidly increasing stock prices more accessible.

The advent of discount brokers made odd lot purchases much less expensive, so investors can now buy just a few shares of a higher priced stock when they don't have much money to invest. Because of this, stock splits are more symbolic than practical these days.

Not every company chooses to institute stock splits. Respected investor Warren Buffett's company Berkshire Hathaway, for example, has never split its stock. In January 2004, one share of Berkshire Hathaway 'A' traded at more than $87,400 a share. Since not many investors can afford to buy one share, Berkshire Hathaway now trades as both Class A and Class B shares.

Berkshire Hathaway Class B shares sell at a much lower price than the Class A shares ($2,915, in this example) but shareholders also have fewer voting rights. While not technically a stock split, the availability of Class B shares offers a similar way for investors to have a chance to invest in a stock that otherwise would be priced beyond their reach.

Reverse stock splits

There are times when a company's fortunes head in the opposite direction. An especially low stock price can be just as discouraging to investors as a tremendously high price. When a stock price dips too low, the company also runs the risk of being delisted by the stock exchange it's traded on, meaning that its shares can no longer be easily bought and sold by investors. That's why a company facing this future may choose to do a reverse stock split.

In a reverse stock split, the shareholder ends up with fewer shares than they started with. A one-for-five stock split,

for example, leaves an investor who previously owned five shares with only one. The share price goes up in a corresponding manner as well, so the investor with five $1 shares now holds one $5 share. Shareholders owning less than five shares in this example would be cashed out completely, since they don't own enough of the old shares to convert into one of the new shares.

The Securities and Exchange Commission (SEC)

The Securities and Exchange Commission (SEC) is a federal agency responsible for establishing and enforcing regulations that protect investors from unfair practices in the securities market. Companies issuing new stocks and bonds to the public are required to file registration information with the SEC, including data on the company, its industry, competitors and management among other topics.

The SEC requires publicly traded companies to regularly report information about earnings, sales and other financial data. These companies must also have their annual financial statements prepared by an outside accounting firm in accordance with generally accepted accounting principles (GAAP).

Price to earnings (P/E) ratio

The price to earnings (P/E) ratio gives you a way to measure and compare a stock's value. Dividing the price of a share by the earnings per share results in a number called the P/E ratio. Higher than average P/E ratios mean that investors judge that the stock will perform well in the future and are willing to pay a higher price than usual to own the stock. Stocks with a lower than average P/E ratio may represent a better value than usual if the stock's earnings and revenues are still strong.

There are different variations on the P/E ratio depending on the earnings you use to calculate it. A current P/E, for example, uses earnings from the last, or trailing, twelve months of earnings. This is the most common way of calculating the P/E ratio. It's

also possible to estimate a future or projected P/E by using forecasted earnings and the current price. Be sure you know the type of earnings and price data you're using when you calculate P/E ratios for your stock analysis. Remember, too, that P/E ratios change every day that the stock price changes.

Upside/downside ratio

The *upside/downside ratio* offers a way of expressing the potential for investment reward over the next five years versus the risk involved. Part of NAIC's Stock Selection Guide, the upside/downside ratio is a comparison between a stock's estimated high and low prices. If you determine based on the information on the SSG that a stock has an upside/downside ratio of three to one, the potential reward is at least three times the potential risk according to your analysis.

Finding Good Prospects

Introduction

Stock screening gives you a way to sort through the tens of thousands of publicly traded companies. Using software to winnow down your choices to fit your requirements is the easiest way, but you can also improve your chances of finding a suitable company without a computer.

This chapter will give you an overview of what to look for in a company. You can find even more helpful information on stock analysis and stock screening in the NAIC Stock Selection Handbook and the NAIC Computerized Investing & the Internet Handbook, two other titles in this educational series.

What type of stock are you looking for?

Your first step in selecting stocks to research in more depth is deciding what type of company to add to your portfolio. In Chapter 4, we discussed diversification and the importance of investing in a variety of types of companies, from smaller to larger companies as well as companies in different sectors and industries.

Diversification is one way to protect your portfolio from deep losses if a particular market industry or sector encounters difficulty. Investors whose portfolios are over weighted in an underperforming sector of the stock market can watch their holdings sustain major losses. Diversifying by investing in companies across a range of industries and market capitalizations can help protect your portfolio from a similar fate. Analyzing your portfolio's holdings and deciding if there are gaps you might want to fill in can give you a few criteria with which to start narrowing down your prospects.

Stock Screening

The vast universe of potential stocks to research can be absolutely overwhelming when you're first starting to invest. Even after you feel like you finally have a handle on the basics of analyzing a stock, how do you choose a few decent prospects out of the many thousands available?

Where to start

If you're looking for stocks to consider researching, you might consider checking out a few NAIC resources for ideas. Keep in mind that **none** of these possible resources contain investment recommendations. What you're searching for are simply a few companies that may or may not be worth analyzing for possible purchase in the future. It's up to you to make that investment decision for yourself, with the help of the NAIC stock selection tools we'll introduce in Chapter 8. Investigate these resources, but don't assume that a company is worth investing in until after you've done your own thorough research.

Don't forget to look at your day-to-day life for inspiration as well. Again, you may want to follow legendary investor Peter Lynch's lead and look at stores you shop at and products and services you use for more potential stocks to research. Almost anything you encounter throughout your day may lead to a publicly traded company worthy of a careful analysis. Besides the world around you, here are a few other places you might turn to for ideas.

Better Investing magazine's "Stock to Study"

Each month, NAIC's *Better Investing* magazine features an in-depth look at a "Stock to Study." As the name makes clear, this article is in no way intended as a recommendation that readers should invest in the featured stock. Instead, this column offers a detailed look at the more interesting or challenging aspects of analyzing a particular stock. Readers can learn more about the specifics of this stock in particular as well as techniques they can use when researching stocks in general.

Each Stock to Study article includes a partially completed Stock Selection Guide (SSG) so you can apply your own judgment to the company and determine if it fits your criteria for addition to your investment portfolio. If you're just beginning to learn to analyze stocks, you may want to complete your own SSG on the Stock to Study each month and read the article thoroughly to practice your newly acquired research skills.

Better Investing magazine "Top 100" list

Better Investing magazine's April issue each year features a Top 100 and Second 100 list of the top investment club stock holdings, based on the results of an annual survey of NAIC member investment clubs. While you shouldn't assume that every company on the list is automatically suitable for investment, you may want to scan the list for companies worthy of further research. You can find this list printed in the April issue of *Better Investing* magazine or online at NAIC's Web Site.

NAIC Low Cost Investment Plan participants

Another list you may want to look through is the corporate participants of NAIC's Low Cost Investment Plan. Inclusion in the plan does not equal an endorsement of the company for investment purposes, but you may very well find a few suitable candidates for more detailed analysis. You can find the list of Low Cost Investment Plan companies in *Better Investing* magazine and at NAIC's Web Site.

Choose an industry

Another strategy you might consider when looking for potential stocks to research is to select an industry to learn more about, then identify a few leading companies in that industry for deeper study. You can find companies listed by industry in the *Value Line Investment Survey*, among other places.

The bare essentials

What are the financial characteristics that might make you look at a company a little more closely? Here are two that you can use to quickly disqualify a prospective company from further research.

Years of publicly traded history

One quick stock-screening tool you can use without a computer is to check how many years a company has been public. As a general rule, beginners should consider companies with a minimum of five years of history as a publicly traded company. This rule can sometimes be waived for companies with less than five years of public history, if there is a longer business operating history. Ten years of data gives you an even better base to start your analysis process with, as ten years of information should show you how a particular company has performed during both up and down periods in the stock market. You can find this information in the company report if you're an NAIC Online Premium Services (OPS) subscriber or in other data sources such as the *Value Line Investment Survey*.

Selecting companies with at least five and preferably ten years of public trading automatically eliminates companies that have just entered the market as an IPO as well as companies that haven't yet established themselves in their market sector. While start-up companies, IPOs and other relatively young companies have a higher potential to bring their investors tremendous returns due in part to rapidly rising earnings, the reverse is also true. Younger or untested companies also have a higher potential for failure, leaving their investors with empty wallets.

Remember our discussion of risk and reward in Chapter 3? This is a perfect example—these companies carry the potential for a higher reward than better established, blue chip companies, but with that potential comes the risk of higher than average losses. Sticking with quality growth companies that have been around the block a few times may mean you're giving up the possibility of higher returns, but in return you're taking on a far lower level of risk.

Increasing earnings over time

After you've identified a few companies with at least the minimum amount of data you're looking for, check the actual earnings. If there aren't any, or if most of the years show negative earnings, that's one less company analysis to worry about finishing. Not only are you looking for a company with more than a few years of financial reports, you're looking for a company with a strong record of positive earnings per share as well. The very best scenario is a company with not only strong earnings per share, but also earnings per share that are increasing year after year.

Screening online

You can screen stocks according to your own or pre-defined requirements online at a variety of Web sites. One free site often used by NAIC members to perform online stock screening is *Reuters Investor*, which you can find at ***www.investor.reuters.com***. You can find more information about online screening in the *NAIC Stock Selection Handbook* and the *NAIC Computerized Investing & the Internet Handbook*.

Screening with software

One other way to screen for stocks using your computer is with NAIC's *Stock Prospector* software along with a subscription to NAIC's Online Premium Services (OPS) data. Prospector includes a wide range of preset screens while also offering you the ability to create screens based on your own parameters. You can learn a little more about Prospector in Chapter 19, and a lot more in the *NAIC Computerized Investing & the Internet Handbook* and the *NAIC Stock Selection Handbook*.

65

NAIC's Stock Selection Tools

Introduction

If you're interested in analyzing individual stocks according to NAIC's investment principles, congratulations! As you continue your education, you'll be joining millions of other investors who have already discovered the rewards of taking control of their own investment portfolio.

This chapter will familiarize you with NAIC's stock selection tools. Available in both paper and software versions, these tools help you organize and complete your stock analysis while following time-tested strategies.

Because this book is merely an introduction to NAIC's investment principles and resources, we won't go into detail about actually using these tools. You can find in-depth instructions and guidance to making the most of these resources in the NAIC Stock Selection Handbook, another in this series of educational books.

Why use stock selection tools?

If you want to learn to analyze individual stocks on your own, there are plenty of methods out there for you to choose from. NAIC's stock selection philosophy concentrates on finding quality growth stocks, then buying them at what you determine to be a reasonable price. If this criteria sounds appealing to you, using NAIC's stock selection tools will make the process much simpler than trying to figure out what information to look for and how to organize and analyze it all on your own.

Another benefit of using these well-established, time tested tools is that you'll be analyzing stocks based on the same types of data and judgment, giving you a consistent framework to follow each time. Consistency is very important, helping to ensure that you're following your own chosen investment philosophy every time you make an investment decision. If you agree with NAIC's basic investment philosophy, then you'll know that you're abiding by guidelines you approve of every time you analyze a stock using NAIC tools.

Remember, though, that these tools are just that—aids to help you in making your own judgments about a company's future prospects for growth. These tools can't make investment decisions for you. They're not meant to give you a black or white answer, but to offer you a way to organize and analyze a company's financial history so that you can determine its investment suitability for yourself.

Again, this chapter can offer only an overview of these valuable tools. Turn to the *NAIC Stock Selection Handbook* for more explanation and detailed instruction.

Fundamental vs. technical analysis

NAIC's stock selection tools use fundamental rather than technical analysis to determine whether a stock might be a good investment choice. Investors using *fundamental analysis* use data from company operations such as the basic operational measures of revenues, expenses and profit, along with other financial data easily accessible from annual reports, SEC filings and data providers such as Value Line. Fundamental analysis studies a company's *fundamentals*, or most basic financial information.

Technical analysis, on the other hand, uses data about the company's stock price movements and trading volume among other items in an attempt to identify patterns that will show the best time to buy and sell the stock. Technical analysts use charts of stock prices and other market statistics to decide if a particular company should be bought or sold. Investors who use technical analysis aren't concerned with a company's earnings, profit margins or other financial results reported by the company, relying instead on investor

Where to get data?

There are a number of places you can turn to for the data you'll need when using NAIC's stock selection tools.

This data includes information about a company's historical financial results, including revenues, expenses and profits. While each data provider gets the same raw data from a company's press releases and SEC filings, the data you get from the provider can vary because each data provider adjusts data according to their own criteria.

Regardless of which data source you use, remember that you shouldn't mix data from different sources unless you understand any differences in how numbers are reported by the data source. If you take some numbers straight from the company's annual report and others from a data provider that adjusts the data in some way, you won't end up with a true picture of the company's financial situation.

sentiment and market trends to aid in their analysis. Technical analysts are sometimes called "chartists" due to their use of charts and tables of market data in their stock studies.

NAIC's philosophy follows a fundamental approach to stock analysis. Investors who use NAIC's stock analysis tools, whether in paper or software form, rely on a company's financial and management history as they go about their research.

Below are descriptions of some of the more popular data sources available to investors. You'll find much more information about selecting and using data sources in the *NAIC Stock Selection Handbook* and the *NAIC Computerized Investing & the Internet Handbook*.

NAIC's Online Premium Services (OPS)

The most convenient data source for NAIC members with computer access is NAIC's Online Premium Services (OPS). OPS data is provided by Standard and Poor's Compustat. An OPS subscription is included with NAIC lifetime memberships. Investment club members, and individual NAIC members may subscribe for a nominal additional annual fee. OPS subscribers simply log in to the NAIC Web Site to view the more than 10,000 company reports available.

OPS data can also be downloaded into any of NAIC's stock selection and stock screening software programs. You can read much more about the source, benefits and many uses of OPS data in the *NAIC Stock Selection Handbook* and the *NAIC Computerized Investing & the Internet Handbook*.

Value Line/S&P

Many NAIC individual and investment club members use stock reports from both the Value Line Investment Survey and Standard & Poor's (S&P). You can find Value Line and S&P reports at many libraries, or subscribe to their online or mail versions.

Company Web sites/ annual reports

You can also get data straight from the source. A company's own Web site will probably provide financial information for at least the past few years. Some companies provide data going back many years, and also have annual reports and other important financial information available for viewing or download.

The SEC Web site is another valuable resource for investors seeking data. You'll find years of past filings from almost every public company in the EDGAR database at *www.sec.gov.*

NAIC's stock study tools

Now comes the fun part— learning about the stock study tools that have proven so valuable to so many NAIC investors over the years. The shining star of NAIC's stock analysis philosophy is the Stock Selection Guide, developed in the 1950's by NAIC co-founder George A.

Nicholson, Jr. The Stock Selection Guide is a step-by-step stock study tool that enables even the most novice investor a proven way to analyze individual stocks in search of good investment prospects. The Stock Selection Guide and NAIC's other stock study tools come in both paper and software versions, giving investors the choice of whichever form is most comfortable and convenient for them to use.

All of NAIC's stock study tools are designed to help investors first understand what makes a stock worth adding to one's portfolio and then learn how to determine if a specific stock meets that criteria. Here's a brief overview of NAIC's stock study tools. Remember that you'll find complete instructions for making the most of these tools in the *NAIC Stock Selection Handbook.*

NAIC's Stock Check List (SCL)

The simplest of NAIC's forms is the Stock Check List (SCL), which gives brand-new investors the opportunity to start a stock analysis before learning the more comprehensive Stock Selection Guide (SSG). The SCL allows you to pursue the first of the three basic tasks of investing— recording and reviewing a company's sales and earnings record as well as its price history. From this data, you can decide whether a stock is a suitable candidate for purchase now or whether it might be a good choice in the future.

While it's a very useful tool for introducing stock selection criteria to novice investors, you shouldn't continue using the SCL beyond your first few stock studies. By then you'll have the basic knowledge you'll need to start to learn the SSG.

NATIONAL ASSOCIATION OF INVESTORS CORPORATION

NAIC ®

INVESTMENT EDUCATION FOR INDIVIDUALS AND CLUBS SINCE 1951

Stock Check List ® *for Beginning Investors*

Company <u>Pfizer</u>

Prepared by <u>BJB</u>

Date <u>06/07/2002</u>

PFE

While Investors are learning to use NAIC's Stock Selection Guide, it is suggested the following Check List be used for each stock considered for investment.

1 PAST SALES RECORD

Sales for most recent year were	(1) $	32259.00
Sales for next most recent year were	(2) $	29574.00
Total of above (1+ 2)	(3) $	61833.00
Figure above divided by 2	(4) $	30916.50
Sales 5 years ago were	(5) $	11306.00
Sales 6 years ago were	(6) $	10021.00
Total of above (5 + 6)	(7) $	21327.00
Figure above divided by 2	(8) $	10663.50
Increase in sales in above period (8 from 4)	(9) $	20253.00
Percentage increase in sales (9 divided by 8)	(10)	189.9 %

CONVERSION TABLE

This % increase in Sales Gives	27	33	46	61	76	93	112	129	148	205	271
This % Compounded Annual Growth Rate	5	6	8	10	12	14	16	18	20	25	30

COMPOUND ANNUAL RATE OF SALES GROWTH WAS <u>24.0</u>%

Look for the percent increase that meets the objective you have set.

2 PAST EARNINGS PER SHARE RECORD

Earnings Per Share for most recent year were	(1) $	1.31
Earnings Per Share for next most recent year were	(2) $	1.02
Total of above (1+ 2)	(3) $	2.33
Figure above divided by 2	(4) $	1.17
Earnings Per Share 5 years ago were	(5)	.50
Earnings Per Share 6 years ago were	(6)	.41
Total of above (5 + 6)	(7)	.91
Figure above divided by 2	(8) $	.46
Increase in Earnings Per Share in above period (8 from 4)	(9) $	.71
Percentage increase in Earnings Per Share (9 divided by 8)	(10)	156.04 %

See Conversion Table above to determine ➡

COMPOUND ANNUAL RATE OF EARNINGS PER SHARE GROWTH WAS <u>21.0</u> %

Earnings Per Share have increased <u>less</u> than sales this period.
(more)   (less)

Explain Apparent Reason for Difference in Sales and Earnings Per Share Growth: <u>nothing unusual</u>

Figure 8-01: A sample NAIC Stock Check List, front and back

Discuss Possible Reasons for Past Growth:

A new product was successful _____✓_____

A cyclical business that experienced recovery_____

A research program has produced several new products or uses for older products _____

Purchase another company _____✓_____

Has taken larger share of business in its field_____

Skill of management _____✓_____

Will Factors Which Produced Past Growth Continue Effective

for the next five years ____✓____ yes, _____ yes, but less effective, _____ no.

3 PRICE RECORD OF THE STOCK

Present Price $__34.58__   Present Earnings Per Share__1.31__

List Last 5 Years	High Price Each Year (A)	Low Price Each Year (B)	Earnings Per Share (C)	Price Earnings Ratio	
				at High (A ÷ C)	at Low (B ÷ C)
1997	26.700	13.400	.570	46.84	23.51
1998	43.000	23.700	.670	64.18	35.37
1999	50.000	31.500	.870	57.47	36.21
2000	49.300	30.000	1.020	48.33	29.41
2001	46.800	34.000	1.310	35.73	25.95
Totals	215.800	132.600	4.440	252.550	150.450
Averages	43.160	26.520	0.888	50.510	30.090
Average of High and Low Price Earnings Averages for the past five years.				40.300	

Present Price is _____higher_____ than high price five years ago.
(higher)   (lower)

Present Price is __29.5%__ % higher that the high price 5 years ago. Compare this figure with the percent sales increase in 1 (10) and percent earnings per share increase in 2 (10).

The price change compares with sales growth and earnings per share growth _____unfavorably_____
(favorably or unfavorably)

This stock has sold as high as the current price in ___4___ of the last 5 years.

In the past five years the stock ___has___ sold at unusually___high___ price earnings ratios.
(has)   (has not)   (high)   (low)

The Present price earnings ratio is__26.397__

In relation to past price earnings ratios the stock is currently

_____ selling at a higher ratio

_____ selling about the same

___✓___ selling lower

The average price earnings ratios of the past might be expected to continue _____
or should be adjusted to__26.40__ high, __18.00__ low.

4 CONCLUSION

1. The past sales growth rate _____does_____ meet our objective.
(does)   (does not)

2. The past earnings per share growth rate_____does_____ meet our objective.
(does)   (does not)

3. Our conclusion has been that possible earnings per share growth rate _____will_____ meet our objective.
in the coming five years.   (will)   (will not)

4. The price of the stock is currently _____too high_____
(acceptable)   (too high)

This form is not meant to give you an adequate analysis of the stock, but is meant to help a beginner ask questions to indicate whether the company is likely to become more valuable and if it can be purchased reasonably. As Investors gain practice, a more thorough study of the stock is suggested using NAIC's Stock Select Guide and Report as a guide.

Stock Comparison Guide

NATIONAL ASSOCIATION OF INVESTORS CORPORATION
NAIC®
INVESTMENT EDUCATION FOR INDIVIDUALS AND CLUBS SINCE 1951

Prepared by _____ BJB, BJB, BJB, BJB, BJB

Date _____ 07/09/2002

NAME OF COMPANY

GROWTH COMPARISONS
(From Section 1 of the NAIC Stock Selection Guide)

	Abbott Lab ABT	JOHNSON & JNJ	Merck MRK	Pfizer PFE	Schering-P SGP
(1) Historical % of Sales Growth	7.9 %	10.5 %	19.4 %	18.1 %	11.9 %
(2) Projected % of Sales Growth	9.0 %	10.0 %	10.0 %	11.0 %	7.0 %
(3) Historical % of Earnings Per Share Growth	11.5 %	14.0 %	13.8 %	19.0 %	16.5 %
(4) Projected % of Earnings Per Share Growth	9.0 %	11.0 %	8.0 %	14.0 %	7.0 %

MANAGEMENT COMPARISONS
(From Section 2 of the NAIC Stock Selection Guide)

		Abbott Lab ABT	JOHNSON & JNJ	Merck MRK	Pfizer PFE	Schering-P SGP
(5) % Profit Margin Before Taxes (Average for last 5 Years)	(2A) Trend	25.8 DOWN	20.1 UP	26.0 DOWN	29.0 UP	30.2 UP
(6) % Earned on Equity (Average for last 5 Years)	(2B) Trend	35.9 DOWN	25.9 DOWN	41.7 UP	36.0 UP	41.4 DOWN
(7) % of Common Owned by Management		0.4	0.1	1.0	1.0	7.0

PRICE COMPARISONS
(From Section 3-5 of the NAIC Stock Selection Guide)

			Abbott Lab ABT	JOHNSON & JNJ	Merck MRK	Pfizer PFE	Schering-P SGP
(8) Estimated Total Earnings Per Share For Next 5 Years			12.26	13.13	19.89	10.32	9.72
(9) Price Range Over Last 5 Years	High (3A) Low (3B)		24.90~57.20	20.80~53.40	39.00~96.70	13.40~50.00	15.90~60.80
(10) Present Price			44.67	62.52	54.65	34.58	24.75
Price Earnings Ratio Range Last 5 Years	(11) Highest	(3D)	33.20	36.00	37.60	35.70	32.30
	(12) Average High	(3D7)	30.70	30.80	33.00	35.70	32.30
	(13) Average	(3-8)	24.90	26.30	27.00	29.60	24.80
	(14) Average Low	(3E7)	19.10	21.80	21.00	23.50	17.40
	(15) Lowest	(3E)	16.50	19.40	17.90	23.50	16.10
(16) Current Price Earnings Ratio	(3-9)		23.80	32.90	17.40	25.20	15.70
Estimated Price Zones	(17) Lower-Buy	(4C2)	33.80~39.80	30.80~41.10	47.10~58.38	24.70~37.65	19.00~24.25
	(18) Middle-Maybe	(4C3)	39.80~51.80	41.10~61.70	58.38~80.92	37.65~63.55	24.25~34.75
	(19) Upper-Sell	(4C4)	51.80~57.80	61.70~72.00	80.92~92.20	63.55~76.50	34.75~40.00
(20) Present Price Range	(4C5)		-Hold-	-Sell-	-Buy-	-Buy-	-Hold-
(21) Upside Downside Ratio	(4D)		1.21	0.30	4.97	4.24	2.65
(22) Current Yield	(5A)		1.84	1.15	2.51	1.27	2.51
(23) Combined Estimated Yield	(5C)		8.08	4.33	16.94	26.35	15.12

OTHER COMPARISONS

		Abbott Lab ABT	JOHNSON & JNJ	Merck MRK	Pfizer PFE	Schering-P SGP
(24) Number of Common Shares Outstanding		1,552.00	3,047.22	2,272.00	6,277.00	1,465.00
(25) Potential Dilution from Debentures, Warrants, Options		None	None	None	0.00	None
(26) Percent Payout	(3G7)	41.00	35.80	43.70	36.40	36.20
(27)		0.0 %	0.0 %	0.0 %	0.0 %	0.0 %
(28)		0.0 %	0.0 %	0.0 %	0.0 %	0.0 %
(29) Date of Source Material		6/4/2002	4/17/2002	6/4/2002	6/4/2002	6/4/2002
(30) Where Traded		NYSE	NYSE	NYSE	NYSE	NYSE

Figure 8-03: A sample NAIC Stock Comparison Guide

NAIC's Stock Comparison Guide (SCG)

After you've completed SSGs for two or more companies in the same industry, you can use NAIC's Stock Comparison Guide (SCG) to help you decide which stock has the best prospects for future growth. As with all of NAIC's stock selection tools, the Stock Comparison Guide is not designed to give you a final answer in black and white. You'll have to make that decision for yourself based on your research and judgment.

In order for the Stock Comparison Guide to be most effective at finding prospective investments, you should only compare a stock to other stocks in the same industry. Earnings and sales rates, pre-tax profit margins and P/E ratios vary widely across industries, making it virtually impossible to correctly compare a restaurant stock, for instance, with a technology stock. Once you've settled on a few promising prospects and are trying to decide which to invest in first, though, you can use the SCG even if these final stocks are in different industries.

MOVING ON...

Now that you've been introduced to NAIC's stock analysis tools, you can start to think about how they might be useful as you construct your own investment portfolio. Don't worry if the terms or concepts we've just glossed over don't make complete sense yet. You'll learn much more about using these tools in the *NAIC Stock Selection Handbook*, and it won't be long before stock analysis becomes second nature to you. Thousands of NAIC investors are proof that you, too, can learn to manage your own investments.

Buying and Selling Stock

Introduction

Ready to make your jump into stocks? You'll need a way to buy them first. Your most obvious option is a brokerage account, but you do have some other alternatives. This chapter will take you through the basics of researching your alternatives, as well as some very general guidelines to get you thinking about why you might want to buy or sell a stock.

Remember that this is just an introduction to the topic. You'll find more details in the NAIC Stock Selection Handbook and the NAIC Computerized Investing & the Internet Handbook.

How to invest in stocks

When it comes time to actually buy or sell a stock, you have a few choices. Most investors choose to open a brokerage account, but there are other options. You'll need to research your choices and decide which one (or more than one) best fit your needs. Here are the most popular alternatives open to you, and the basics you should consider before making a choice.

Full-service brokerage

It used to be that the only type of broker an individual could work with was one employed by a full-service brokerage. Full-service brokerages such as Merrill Lynch and A.G. Edwards employ analysts who make investment recommendations based on their research. Investors pay higher commissions than they would at a discount brokerage, but usually receive more personalized attention in addition to purchase recommendations from their particular broker. Only you can decide if this type of extra attention is worth the higher expenses.

Several full-service brokerages have come under fire due to the potential conflicts of interest between their stock analyst and investment banking divisions. If you choose to use a full-service broker, be sure to ask your broker how he or she is compensated. If they come to you with stock recommendations, you should ask why they're recommending that particular stock and whether or not they receive any special compensation or other reward if their clients end up buying it.

Most brokers aren't paid based on how well your portfolio performs, but rather on how many transactions they complete for your account among other criteria. For this reason, a full-service broker is more a salesperson than a financial planner in most cases. You're in the process of learning to make your own stock selection judgments, so there's not much reason to pay a broker to do what you can do for yourself.

Discount/online brokerage

Most discount brokerages are also considered online brokerages, so we'll consider them the same entity in this book. Using an online brokerage doesn't mean you'll be day trading or frequently buying and selling stocks with your home computer. It just means that you're able to conduct all of your brokerage business online in addition to over the phone or potentially in person if the brokerage has a local office in your area.

Discount brokerage firms offer commissions much lower than those traditionally offered by full-service brokerages. In return for these lower commissions and expenses, you'll be on your own when it comes to investment recommendations. Discount brokerages don't generally offer any guidance as to which stock you should buy or even what percentage of your portfolio should be made up of stocks in the first place. That shouldn't be too big of a problem if your goal is to learn to research and choose your own investments anyway. Many full-service brokerages have their own discount brokerage arms, which

you may want to investigate if you're already a full-service account holder.

The level of services offered and expenses charged can vary greatly from one discount brokerage to another. You'll want to compare features and expenses before deciding which brokerage best suits your needs. Some of the services offered include free check writing and automatic dividend reinvestment. You should shop around until you find the firm that offers most of the features you're looking for. If you're in an investment club, for example, choosing a brokerage with check writing privileges can mean that your club won't need a separate account with a local bank if the club needs check writing ability. You can find resources to help you select the best brokerage

for your needs in the Online Resource Guide at the end of this book.

Dividend Reinvestment and Direct Share Purchase Plans

A Dividend Reinvestment Plan (often referred to as a DRIP) is a way for you to purchase more shares of a stock you already own by directly reinvesting any dividends you receive from the stock. Many, though not all, dividend-paying companies offer DRIPs, and fees can vary widely from plan to plan. Most plans require that investors already own a minimum number of shares in the company (typically one to five shares).

If you're considering enrolling in a particular DRIP, be sure to request and fully read the plan's prospectus so that you're aware of any charges for purchases and sales, as well as for issuing

or transferring stock certificates. Many brokerage accounts will allow you to reinvest dividends for free, so look into that option as well before you enroll in a DRIP plan that charges purchase or reinvestment fees. Those brokerage accounts that allow dividend reinvestment do not have the optional cash investment feature that DRIPs offer. When you add to holdings with an additional cash investment, regular brokerage commissions are charged.

Another way to buy stock is directly from the company, through a Direct Stock Purchase (DSP) plan. Such plans are similar to DRIPs but they allow investors to buy their initial shares through the company rather than using a brokerage firm as a middleman. DSPs may require a minimum initial investment and may charge commissions on each purchase (though these are typically much lower than you'd pay in you invested through a brokerage). DSPs usually allow investors to reinvest dividends automatically as well.

NAIC's Low Cost Investment Plan

Many, though not all, DRIPs require that investors own at least one share in the company before they can enroll in the DRIP. Buying one share of stock from a full-service or discount broker can be prohibitively expensive due to the commission cost. NAIC's *Low Cost Investment Plan* gives NAIC members a way to purchase the first share of over 130 different companies and be automatically enrolled in their DRIP or Direct Purchase Plan at the same time. You can learn more about the Low Cost Plan in Chapter 19 as well as in the *NAIC Computerized Investing & the Internet Handbook.*

Retirement accounts

You may also have the option of investing in individual stocks in your retirement account. Some 401(k) and 403(b) plans may offer this option, but there's no guarantee you'll be able to invest in anything other than mutual funds. (If this is the case, you'll learn more about NAIC's mutual fund educational resources and analysis tools in Part III of this book).

Even if you can't invest directly in stocks through your employer's retirement plan, if you're eligible to invest in an IRA, you can choose to open your IRA through a brokerage house. This will allow you to invest in individual stocks in your brokerage IRA.

Another brokerage option

If you're looking to regularly invest in individual stocks but want to keep your commission costs as low as possible, you may want to investigate a newer type of investment account. Companies such as ShareBuilder *(www.sharebuilder.com)* and BuyandHold *(www.buyandhold.com)* offer investors an alternative to traditional discount brokerages. You can invest smaller amounts of money in a wider variety of stocks each month yet pay only a relatively small monthly fee instead of separate commissions for each stock purchase.

Account holders can set up automatic investment plans (similar to corporate dividend reinvestment and direct stock purchase plans) where they can set up a portfolio of stocks to be purchased regularly. If you're interested in this type of investment option, research the companies that offer them carefully, paying close attention to any restrictions such as the frequency of investment purchases and fees for sales and lack of account activity.

Investment clubs

One other way to invest regularly in individual stocks while learning more about stock analysis at the same time is to join an investment club. Part IV will give you an overview of the benefits of club membership as well as details on how to join or start a club of your own.

Choosing a broker

One of your first steps as a beginning investor is to open an account with a brokerage firm. With so many brokerages out there, how do you know where to start? Below we've listed some of the most important qualities to look for in a broker. You'll find more tips on choosing a brokerage (especially online brokerages) in the *NAIC Computerized Investing & the Internet Handbook.*

WHAT TO LOOK FOR IN A BROKER:

Web site: If you plan to make transactions online (a great way to reduce commission costs at many brokerages), test drive a few brokerage sites first to make sure they're fast as well as easy to use.

Customer service: Even if you intend to use the brokerage's Web site for all your transactions, you're sure to have some reason to call customer service at some point. Try calling to request new account information, paying attention to how long you have to wait for your call to be answered and how well the customer service representative answers your questions. Also check to see if there's a local office near you, if that's something you find important.

Research resources: Investigate the types of online or other types of research tools the brokerage offers to see if they meet your needs.

Documentation: Although you may not be able to see them until you're a customer, try to check out the brokerage's account statements to make sure they're easily understandable and give you all the information you're interested in.

Access to recent and historic statements online: Check to see if you can view or download current or past account statements and tax information online.

Commissions and other expenses: While you don't want to choose a brokerage simply based on commission costs, you do want to ensure that they're not overly high. The same goes with account expenses. Make sure you won't be nickel and dimed by charges for account inactivity, closing or transferring the account, dividend reinvestment, and mailing trade confirmations, for instance. You can often find a complete commission and fee schedule at a brokerage's Web site. If you can't locate it on your own, call customer service and request a written copy.

Minimum initial deposit: Some brokerages allow you to open an account with no minimum deposit while others require thousands of dollars be deposited at opening. Choose a brokerage that fits your initial deposit capabilities.

Investment club considerations: Investment clubs have their own set of brokerage requirements to be aware of, including online access to statements, a dual password system so all members can view portfolio information but only approved members can buy or sell, etc. Check the *NAIC Investment Club Operations Handbook* for what to look for in a club-friendly broker.

Placing an order

Once you've chosen a brokerage firm and have opened and funded your account, you're all set up to actually buy a stock once you identify a quality prospect. Placing the order isn't quite as simple as picking up the phone or going online to place your order. You also need to know what type of order you want to place, and how order pricing works.

Bid vs. ask price

The *bid* is an indication of the price you can sell at, and the *ask* is the price you can purchase at. The difference between these two prices is called the spread. Stocks that are very popular or heavily traded commonly have a very narrow spread (meaning that the buying and selling prices are almost identical). Thinly traded stocks (i.e. very low volume of trading) may have a very wide *spread*, meaning the buying and selling prices may be dollars apart. Each transaction has the possibility of changing the bid and ask prices.

Market order

If you want to buy or sell stock at the best price currently available, place a *market order*. If the market is open, your order will be sent to the market and executed (completed) immediately at the current price.

You may want to be careful about placing a market order when the market is closed, however. Such an order will be executed as soon as the market opens. If bad or good news is announced between the time that you place your order and the time that the order is executed, you could find yourself buying at a price much higher than the last closing price or selling at a price far below what you expected.

It's best to place a market order when the market is open, and after you've checked the current bid or ask price to ensure that it's in a range you're comfortable with.

Limit order

If you want to specify the price at which you'll buy or sell shares (especially if you're placing your order when the market is closed), place a *limit order*. This will reduce the risk that you'll pay more than you wanted on purchases or receive less than you expected on sales.

Be aware that many brokerages charge a higher commission for limit orders than for market orders. Also, it's possible to miss out on a stock you want to buy completely by using a limit instead of market order. The stock price may come to within pennies of your limit order price without meeting it, then move up, leaving your order unfilled even though the price was so close to your limit.

Day vs. good-til-cancelled (GTC) order

If you're considering selling a stock but only if it reaches $60 a share on the day you place your order, place a *day* order with this limit. If the stock price doesn't reach the specified price that day, the order will automatically expire at the market close.

To keep the order to stay standing for days, weeks or months until the stock either reaches that specific share price or until you reach the brokerage's order expiration date (typically sixty days), place a limit order that's *good-til-cancelled* (GTC). The order will stay on the books until it's either filled or cancelled by the brokerage.

If you do place a GTC order, be sure that you check the stock price and status of your order from time to time so that you're not caught by surprise if an order you placed a month ago and then forgot about is executed.

Cash vs. margin accounts

When it comes time to buy stocks, you have two choices for paying for your purchases. You can open a *cash account*, meaning that you'll either have money already in your account or that you'll deposit money to cover your transactions within three days of the trade date (called T+3 after the SEC requirement regulating this type of transaction).

Another option is to borrow the money to pay for your stock purchases by opening a

margin account with your brokerage. The brokerage will allow you to buy stocks on margin, which means that the brokerage is giving you a loan to pay for the stocks you buy.

You should steer clear of buying on margin for a variety of reasons. Not only will you be paying interest to your broker for this loan, but if the value of the stock you purchased on margin drops a certain percentage below the purchase price, you could be subject to a margin call. In this case, you would be required to immediately pay back the entire amount you owe to the brokerage. Many investors have incurred deep losses after they've unexpectedly received margin calls and found that the only way they can pay back their loan is to sell off the stock at a loss.

A little something about selling

Knowing when to sell is equally as important as knowing when or how to buy. With buying, once you're confident that you've found a quality company and that the price is attractive, all you need to do is decide to go ahead with the purchase. You'll find guidance on knowing when to sell in the NAIC Using Portfolio Management Wisdom Handbook, but here are a few of the more straightforward reasons you may decide to sell a stock.

You need the money

If you need cash, obviously your decision isn't so much to sell as it is what to sell. You'll find guidance on this issue in the NAIC Using Portfolio Management Wisdom Handbook.

Fundamentals are declining

You may have bought a particular stock in part because both earnings and sales were increasing year after year. Once you own the stock, you'll continue to regularly follow these financial details as part of your portfolio management routine. If you notice declining fundamentals, you'll want to do more research into the cause of the decline. If you don't like the reasons you discover for the downturn, it's probably time to sell.

Fraud or scandal

There are times when you'll decide to sell a stock on bad news even if that means taking a huge loss. This is a personal decision and one you should deliberate over carefully. If strong evidence of fraud or scandal concerning a company you own comes to light, you may decide to wash your hands of the whole thing before the news gets even worse. Some investors have little patience for corporate misbehavior.

They'd rather sell immediately and then invest in another company whose management they can trust.

While we all hope that the companies we invest in are run by ethical people according to sound business practices, there's no way to ever be completely protected from the potential for fraud. It's a good idea to think through your possible reactions to bad news concerning one of the companies in your portfolio, so that in the unlikely event that you're faced with this terrible situation someday, you'll already know if you're going to hang on in hopes of better news or bail out right away to cut your losses.

Portfolio rebalancing

Sometimes a stock performs so far beyond your expectations that it becomes a much greater percentage of your portfolio than you're comfortable holding. While there are certainly worse problems in life than a highly profitable stock, this is one of those times you'll need to make an important portfolio management decision.

When one stock makes up a larger percentage of your portfolio than others, you run the risk of greater than average losses if that stock's price takes a sudden tumble. Even if you think the price will continue to rise, it may be prudent to sell part of the holding and invest the proceeds in another stock to bring your portfolio holdings back into a more healthy balance. You'll want to ask yourself if the stock is likely to continue to appreciate so that you reach your individual company and portfolio total return, or if another stock might be a better value now.

Selling a winning stock may leave you conflicted; no one likes the prospect of leaving money on the table. But you don't need to sell the entire position, unless you judge that the stock is highly overvalued and you'd rather switch to another stock with greater growth potential. Again, you can find more guidance on this and similar situations in the *NAIC Using Portfolio Management Wisdom Handbook*.

PART THREE:
Investing in Mutual Funds

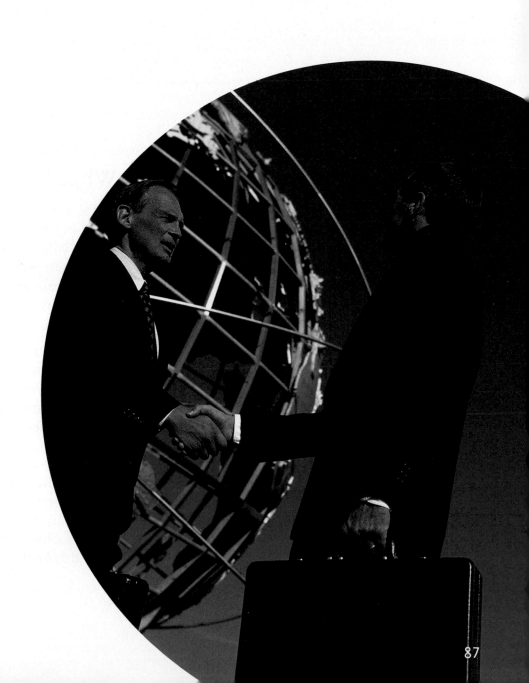

Mutual Fundamentals

Introduction

Mutual funds offer a convenient way to invest in a portfolio of stocks, bonds, money market funds, and even real estate. This convenience doesn't mean that you can overlook the importance of researching

potential mutual funds before you buy, though. In this chapter you'll learn about different types of mutual funds and the reasons you might want to invest in funds.

What is a mutual fund?

In the simplest of definitions, a mutual fund pools the money of many investors into one fund whose management then purchases investments according to the mutual fund's *investment philosophy*. Each shareholder owns a proportionate share of the fund equal to the money that they have invested.

Mutual funds can be made up of stocks, bonds, cash (money market funds), or a variety of other investment vehicles. Funds can also be a combination of these assets, such as balanced funds that invest in a specific proportion of stocks and bonds or other fixed-income investments. Chapter 11 will introduce you to some of the major types of mutual funds, but we'll concentrate almost exclusively on stock and bond funds in this book.

A history of mutual funds

But before we get to all that, a little background. The first *open-end* mutual fund, Massachusetts Investors Trust (MIT) was created in 1924. MIT allowed investors to buy and sell fund shares at will, and with far lower expenses than the typical investment trusts investors had access to at that time. Expenses dropped even lower in 1928, when Boston money management firm Scudder Stevens & Clark opened the first *no-load* (meaning no sales charge) mutual fund.

The Securities Act of 1933 required that mutual funds make a *prospectus* available to potential shareholders (more on the value of the prospectus in Chapter 14). The 1950s brought further growth to the increasingly popular mutual fund industry as investing giants John Templeton and T. Rowe Price opened funds. The year 1975 saw the introduction of both 401(k) plans and the *discount brokerage* industry such as Charles Schwab. A year later, Vanguard revolutionized mutual funds with the introduction of the first *index fund*. More changes came to the mutual fund industry with the introduction of Individual Retirement Accounts (IRAs) in 1981.

Today there are over 8,300 mutual funds, with more than six trillion dollars total invested in them. You can't open a financial magazine without seeing page after page of fund advertisements. Mutual funds are a way of life for millions of investors now.

Mutual fund structure

A mutual fund is made up of a pool of money contributed by all of the fund's shareholders, invested in whatever assets the fund's investment philosophy dictates. Legally, funds are structured as corporations or business trusts. As a shareholder, you own a proportionate share of the fund in the same way that you own a proportionate share of a company when you own common stock.

Mutual funds can be actively managed, where a manager or more frequently these days, a management team, chooses the investments, or passively managed, like index funds where the investment decisions are automated based on the index the fund is attempting to imitate.

Unlike owning individual stocks, when you own a mutual fund you don't usually get to vote on matters the way you would by proxy or at the annual shareholder meetings. You trust the fund's management to make these decisions for you. Mutual fund owners can't tell the management of actively managed funds which investments to buy, for example, though there are times when shareholders are given an opportunity to vote on leadership issues. Shareholders can still voice concerns to management, of course, but can't be guaranteed their opinions will be accepted.

Just as holders of individual stocks do, mutual fund shareholders also receive regular statements containing earnings reports, listings of fund holdings and fund management's outlook for the future.

A mutual fund vocabulary lesson

While all mutual funds calculate their *net asset value* the same way and share the same basic legal structure, there are often more differences than similarities when it comes to other comparisons. These are some of the most important mutual fund terms you should know.

Net asset value (NAV)

Stock prices fluctuate throughout the trading day based on supply and demand. Most mutual funds, on the other hand, are valued only once a trading day, after the market has closed. This valuation is based on the fund's net asset value, or NAV.

The chart below shows how the NAV is derived, but really it's a very simple process. The NAV is the current market value of all of the mutual fund's holdings (investments plus any cash) minus its liabilities, then divided by the total number of outstanding shares in the fund. Sound similar to how you calculated your own net worth a few chapters ago? It is, except that the total net worth is then divided into tiny pieces representing the value of each share in the fund.

In the example below, that day's NAV is $9.90, which is the amount per share you would receive if you'd sold any shares earlier that day. The NAV isn't always the price you pay to buy a fund, however, because there might also be sales charges added on to the cost.

Investment objective

Like your own personal investment philosophy, a mutual fund's *investment objective* (found in the fund prospectus, which you should analyze before investing) explains the basis for the fund manager's investment decisions. Is the fund aggressively seeking a high return by investing in high-risk technology stocks, or does it follow a more conservative route by seeking to replicate a large market index? It's important for you to know the fund's stated investment objective so you can decide if it's the right type of fund to help you meet your own financial objectives.

Investment style

There are three major mutual fund investment styles: growth, value and blend (core) style. You'll find these terms used by mutual fund data sources such as Morningstar (more on mutual fund data sources in Chapter 14). Managers of growth style funds seek out companies with above-average sales and earnings growth. Value-oriented managers buy companies that appear undervalued based on certain measurements. Managers of blend style funds mix the two styles, following a growth approach combined with the addition of undervalued companies.

NAV FORMULA

The net asset value is the current total market value of the portfolio holdings plus cash holdings...minus its liabilities...divided by the number of shares outstanding.

Shown as an equation:

Portfolio Assets – Liabilities/Total # of Shares = NAV

Say the total of all Growth Fund XYZ's holdings are worth $10,000,000 at close of trading today. The fund's liabilities total $100,000 (one percent) and there are one million shares outstanding.

$10,000,000 – $100,000/ 1,000,000 = $9.90 NAV

Fees and expenses

Mutual funds can charge a variety of fees in addition to regular operating expenses. You should fully identify all fees and expenses charged by a fund you're considering investing in.

No-load funds

Many mutual funds carry an upfront sales charge, also called a *front-end load*. While there are several different types of loads, all loads compensate brokers, financial planners or insurance agents for providing investment advice. There isn't anything wrong with getting investment advice, but as with many other services, it comes at a cost.

Paying a front-end load when you purchase a mutual fund means that your investment dollars are reduced by the same percentage as the sales charge. If you invest $10,000 in a fund that charges a six percent load, for example, $600 of your money goes to the persons involved in the marketing (sales) of the shares instead of into your investment account. By investing in a no-load fund, all $10,000 goes to work for you. Put another way, if you invest in a fund with a six percent sales charge, that fund has to earn 6.38% more than a no-load fund just to bring your investment value back up to where it started.

In addition to front-end loads, mutual funds can also charge back-end loads, where you pay a certain percentage when you withdraw funds within a specified period of time after your purchase. *Level load* funds charge an ongoing load—usually about one percent for the entire period of time an investor owns shares in the fund. *12b-1* fees (see below) can also eat away at your investment dollars.

Studies have shown that loaded funds don't outperform no-load funds. With thousands of no-load funds available, chances are very good that you can find a superior no-load fund that will meet your investing needs.

Management fees and operating expenses

All mutual funds incur management fees and operating expenses, which are passed along to the shareholders. These fees—collectively known as the expense ratio—are paid to the fund company for management of the portfolio and for other services such as maintaining fund records, and publishing statements and regular fund reports.

In plain terms, the expense ratio expresses the percentage of assets that you as a fund investor pay for fund management and operating expenses. The expense ratio is deducted from your assets. For example, if you invested $10,000 in a fund with a one percent expense ratio, you would pay the fund company $100 out of your investment assets each and every year you owned fund shares. If the value of your fund shares rose to $20,000, you would pay $200 in expense ratio costs.

Annual charges average from under .25 percent to 1.5 percent of the fund's total asset value, but can be as high as three percent for some funds. Many index funds (described in more detail below) carry lower expense ratios than actively managed funds.

12b-1 fee and other expenses

Named for the SEC rule that allows it, a 12b-1 fee is simply a marketing fee that includes expenses for advertising and sales literature. A fund with annual 12b-1 fees in excess of .25 percent cannot be considered *no-load*. Other expenses a fund can charge include telephone service, costs of a dividend reinvestment plan, postage expenses and more.

Expense ratio

If you find yourself choosing between two mutual funds that are otherwise similar in performance and return, you may decide to let the funds' expense ratios influence your final decision. The expense ratio is a way of describing the relationship between a fund's expenses and the fund's net assets. The expense ratio does not include account-based expenses such as brokerage commissions, sales loads, account maintenance fees, redemption fees and exchange fees.

The SEC requires that mutual funds provide a three-, five- and 10-year expense projection to shareholders as well as to prospective investors. This projection includes all expenses and gives investors a way to accurately compare load and no-load funds as well as funds of differing sizes. This kind of information is very important to prospective investors because every extra dollar of expenses a fund pays out reduces the fund's overall return.

Of course, you can't choose a mutual fund simply based on its expense ratio. Expenses are only one piece of the picture you need to consider, along with the fund's investment style, risk, performance and how well the fund's investment objective matches your own financial goals.

Redemption fees

Purchasing a mutual fund with redemption fees means that you may be charged a fee if you sell (redeem) any of your fund shares. Redemption fees typically last for a short, specific period of time (often 30, 180 or 365 days). Some redemption fees can last up to five years. Redemption fees can also be charged if you exchange funds within a fund family. These fees are always put back into the fund's assets—they aren't paid to the management company as a back-end load.

Mutual fund managers may also use redemption fees as a way to discourage market timers, investors who hop in and out of mutual funds trying to capture a quick gain. Excessive investment movements by market timers can be disruptive to a mutual fund. Since these types of investors can also cause a fund's operating expenses to increase due to higher transaction costs, fund managers of vulnerable funds may use redemption fees as a protective measure.

Brokerage commissions

In the same way that you pay brokerage commissions when you buy and sell individual stocks, mutual funds must also pay these expenses. You can find out how much a fund has paid out in brokerage commissions by reading the fund's annual report (see Chapter 12 for more information on mutual fund annual reports). Brokerage fees aren't included in a fund's expense ratio. They are charged to shareholders on top of other fees and expenses in the fund expense ratio.

Fund management styles

Actively managed funds

An actively managed mutual fund is one in which actual people, a fund manager or management team, make the investment decisions. You can research the fund managers, including their past investment results, using information you can often get from the mutual fund company or in the fund's prospectus. Many investors look for a record of long-term management success before they'll choose a particular mutual fund.

Index funds

Index funds are mutual funds that attempt to reproduce the holdings and performance of a specific market index. For example, there are index funds that aim to replicate the investments in the Standard & Poor's 500 (S&P 500), an index of 500 large-cap companies. You can buy index funds for virtually every major stock market, as well as bond market, index.

In most cases, any new money that an index fund receives from investors on a particular day is invested proportionately into the portfolio holdings of whichever index the fund is tracking. For example, if a fund tracking the S&P 500 received one million dollars in new money in a certain trading day, a computer program would automatically allocate shares of that money into each of the stocks represented in the index.

However, there are some index funds that invest in very broad market indexes, such as an index representing the entire stock market, that don't actually purchase all the companies in the index because to do so would be prohibitively expensive. Instead, they employ a sampling technique whereby some, but not all, of the smallest companies in the index are representatively included in the

fund. If stocks are removed or added to a particular index (an infrequent but still potential event), the fund would sell all shares of the stock being dropped or buy shares of the new addition.

Because index funds are passively managed and investment decisions are largely automated, they tend to incur much lower operating expenses than actively managed funds. This can often make an important difference when calculating a fund's total return. Index fund fans like to point out that the large majority of actively managed mutual funds don't beat the broad market indexes each year, so there's no reason to pay the higher expenses of these funds only to receive lower returns in the end.

Open vs. closed-end funds

Most investment funds are open ended, which means that there is no set number of shares outstanding. This type of fund is also called a "mutual fund." Any investor can invest at any time and in unlimited quantities, as long as the fund is open to new investment dollars and any minimum initial investment is met.

Closed-end funds are similar to individual stocks in that there is a set number of shares that can be bought or sold. Shares of these funds trade like a stock.

Due to differences in supply and demand, the price you pay for a share of a closed-end fund can often be higher or lower than the fund's net asset value. If the market is weak, shares in a closed-end fund may sell at a discount. When the market is strong, shares may sell at a premium. In order to buy a share in a closed-end fund, there has to be a shareholder willing to sell his shares to you.

This can lead to one problem with closed-end funds—the potential for a lack of liquidity. If shareholders don't want to sell their shares, new investors might not be able to buy in except by paying a very high premium compared to the fund's NAV. Conversely, if the fund is not doing well, shareholders may have a hard time finding any buyer at all for their shares.

Closed mutual funds

Not to be confused with closed-end funds, a closed mutual fund is one that's no longer accepting new money from investors (or in some circumstances, only accepting investments from current shareholders). Mutual fund managers will close funds for different reasons, but usually funds close to new investors when they become too large to manage efficiently. If a fund grows too large, it can be difficult for fund management to pursue the fund's stated objectives. A mutual fund manager may choose to close a fund to new money for a period of months or years to prevent the fund from becoming unwieldy.

NAIC's Four Principles of Mutual Fund Investing

The same four basic investing principles you first encountered in Chapter 2 can be applied to mutual funds as easily as they are to individual stocks.

1 **Invest regularly, and for the long term**

Mutual funds make it easy for shareholders to invest regularly. Most fund families offer investors an opportunity to set up automatic investment plans that will regularly deduct funds from your checking or savings account

to invest in your choice of mutual funds. You can also set up plans to deduct investment money automatically from your paycheck.

Investing regularly, through up markets and down, is one of the keys to successful long-term investing (as long as you're researching your investment choices carefully first, of course). As we mentioned earlier, *dollar cost averaging* allows you to accumulate more shares in your chosen investment because you buy more shares when the fund's NAV is low and less when it's high. When you choose quality no-load mutual funds that invest in growth stocks and then hold these funds for the long term, you're giving yourself the best possible chance to create a strong, healthy portfolio.

❷ Reinvest earnings, dividends and profits

Reinvesting your mutual fund dividends and capital gains couldn't be easier. Simply request that all fund distributions (such as dividends and capital gains) be reinvested and your money will continue to work for you after being reinvested in your chosen

mutual funds. If you want to reinvest earnings and dividends in other funds or into a money market fund, you can easily have them automatically transferred elsewhere as well.

By reinvesting your dividends and other fund distributions, you allow them to compound. As we illustrated earlier in Chapter 2, compounding can greatly increase your investment return over time.

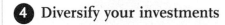

❸ Buy growth stock mutual funds

Remember when we talked about average annual returns for different types of investments in Chapter 2? Historically, the best return has come from investing in stocks. Investing in quality stock mutual funds can produce similar results as well. NAIC's mutual fund tools can help you identify mutual funds that invest in high quality growth stocks. Just as you look for companies with consistent growth in earnings, you'll want to look for funds that invest in this type of company as well.

❹ Diversify your investments

Diversification is an attempt to minimize risk. As we explained earlier, diversification means making sure all your eggs aren't in one basket. Mutual funds allow you to diversify by investing in a wider range of stocks than you can easily (or affordably) replicate in your own portfolio of individual stocks. You can also diversify your mutual funds even if you're trying to invest primarily in growth stock funds by choosing funds that focus on large-, mid- or small-cap stocks.

CHAPTER ELEVEN

Finding a Place for Funds

Introduction

Earlier in this book we praised the virtues of investing in individual stocks. Stocks aren't the only investment option to consider, though. Mutual funds offer another way to invest, whether you use them instead of or in addition to individual stocks.

Mutual funds are a vehicle most appropriate for those who invest on their own, not through an investment club. Investment clubs, which we cover in more detail in Part IV, offer some of the same benefits of mutual funds but without charging a

management fee. Mutual funds aren't usually an appropriate investment for most investment clubs (with the possible exception of international mutual funds for clubs that want exposure to foreign investments).

The key to investing in mutual funds is knowing how to select the best fund for your situation out of the options you have available, which we'll explain in more detail in Chapter 14. In the meantime, here are a few of the more common reasons for investing in mutual funds.

No other choice

One of the most common reasons that investors choose mutual funds is simply because they don't have any other choice. If you have a retirement plan through your employer, mutual funds may be the only investment option your employer provides. The same is true with Section 529 college savings plans as well as other investment accounts.

Investing in mutual funds requires research and planning similar to what you do when investing in individual stocks. Depending on your situation, you most likely have at least a few funds to choose from so you do have some freedom to select the funds that best meet your investment requirements. With a little research into your choices, you can select the funds with the best chances for helping you reach your financial goals. NAIC's mutual fund tools can help you identify the most promising funds from all of your options.

Diversification

Another reason for investing in mutual funds is instant diversification (see Chapter 2 for more on diversification). Buying shares in a single stock mutual fund can give you exposure to potentially thousands of different stocks, depending on the type of fund in which you invest. A $50 monthly contribution, for example, can allow you to invest in dozens of different stocks at once, something that might take years to accomplish if you were investing solely in individual stocks.

Sector exposure

Mutual funds also offer easy exposure to sectors of the stock market that can be difficult for beginning investors to analyze. If you're interested in the energy sector or banking industry within the financial sector, for example, you might find them a little harder to research or analyze than companies in other sectors of the stock market. By purchasing shares of a mutual fund (after doing the appropriate research to select such a fund, of course) that purchases only stocks in that sector, you can bring these types of stocks into your portfolio while letting the fund's managers do the actual individual stock analysis for you.

Sector funds also provide a convenient way for individuals and possibly even investment clubs to add foreign investments to their portfolio. It can be difficult for investors to analyze individual international stocks because not every country requires companies to disclose the information necessary to complete an SSG. By choosing a reputable international mutual fund, you can let the fund's management do the financial detective work for you while still adding an additional type of diversification to your portfolio.

Keep in mind that sector funds can be extremely volatile, flourishing when their particular sector is in favor in the market, and plunging when it's not. If you lack a strong stomach for volatility, it might be better to stick with a more broadly based fund that invests in a number of market sectors.

Small investment amounts

If you don't have much money to invest each month, buying small amounts of individual stocks can at times become very expensive if brokerage commissions eat away a large percentage of your total investment dollars. Many no-load mutual funds allow you to invest as little as $50 a month, and if you don't pay a sales charge, every dollar of your investment goes right to work for you.

You can also set up automatic investments with many mutual fund companies without making a large initial investment. This makes investing automatic because you can arrange for your monthly investment amount to be transferred directly from your paycheck or bank account into your mutual fund account. It's hard to match that convenience, as long as you've researched your chosen fund before investing in it.

Convenience

Even if you're not using an automatic investment plan, investing in a mutual fund is quite simple. In Chapter 13, which covers this topic in more detail, you'll learn how easy it can be to purchase funds and arrange for automatic reinvestment of all dividend and capital gain distributions.

choosing a particular fund. There's usually not a large difference in returns between money market funds, but the lower the fund expenses, the higher your return should be because you're paying less to the fund for management fees and other expenses. Even a difference as small as .25 percent can add up over time.

Stock funds

These are mutual funds that invest primarily in the stocks of publicly held companies. Stock funds can also invest in cash and bonds depending on the fund, so it's in your best interest to read the mutual fund prospectus carefully to make sure that the stock fund you're considering really is investing primarily in stocks. (We'll discuss more about reading a mutual fund prospectus in Chapter 13.)

Stock funds make money the same way individual stocks do, through share price increases and through dividend payouts. Stock funds can focus on investing in specific types of companies, such as only large-cap or small-cap companies. When

you research stock mutual funds for potential purchase, be sure you're comparing funds with the same investment objective and that invest in companies with similar characteristics.

Bond funds

You've probably already figured this one out on your own, but bond mutual funds invest in—bonds. Types of bond funds range from those investing in high-quality government bonds to those investing in high-risk corporate junk bonds and every type of bond in between.

Balanced funds

Balanced funds offer an opportunity to invest in a mixed bag of stocks and bonds, usually with a set proportion of 60 percent in stock, 40 percent in bonds. The actual proportion and investment mix varies from fund to fund and can be found in the fund's prospectus.

Growth funds

Growth funds invest in stocks with potential for capital appreciation (another name for an increase in share price). Growth fund managers look for companies with increasing sales and earnings, the same characteristics investors look for when investing in stocks using NAIC principles.

Money market funds

A share in a money market fund represents ownership in a pool of short-term securities that pay interest. Money market funds are available in taxable and tax-exempt versions. Many money market funds offer the convenience of free check writing, though they may require a minimum check amount and limit the number of checks you can write each month.

Carefully research the expenses a mutual fund charges before

Growth fund managers, however, don't employ the exact same methods for spotting growth companies that NAIC investors do. Don't make the mistake of assuming that every growth fund invests according to NAIC methodology.

Aggressive growth funds

These funds aim for maximum gains by taking larger risks than regular growth funds. Aggressive growth fund managers seek these gains by investing in stocks with potential, rather than actual, earnings growth. These are often smaller companies in a currently popular industry.

Aggressive funds tend to have very high portfolio turnover rates, meaning that the fund managers buy and sell portfolio holdings frequently. While it's possible that this type of trading may lead to higher returns, it's almost a certainty that active trading will lead to higher brokerage commissions and capital gain taxes for shareholders (important to know if you hold the fund in a taxable account).

Stock income funds

Stock income funds invest in stocks that pay high dividends. This type of fund is attractive to investors who want some

exposure to stocks and are willing to give up higher growth potential for higher income.

Growth and income funds

These funds hold both growth and income stocks and sometimes bonds as well.

International funds

International funds invest in stocks, and sometimes bonds, from countries outside of the United States. Investors often choose international funds to provide economic, geographic and currency-related diversification. If the United States economy is experiencing a down period, for example, international fund investors hope that other economies around the world are more robust.

Global funds

Global funds invest anywhere in the world, *including* the United States. Fund management usually sets a maximum percentage of foreign versus domestic investments.

Real Estate Investment Trust (REIT) funds

REIT funds give investors a way to invest in a variety of real estate positions, from residential to office to retail.

Sector funds

Sector funds focus on specific parts of the stock market, either an industry (such as technology) or even smaller, more specific segments of a larger industry (such as computer chip makers).

Something New: Exchange Traded Funds (ETFs)

Exchange traded funds (ETFs) are not mutual funds, but rather are similar to stocks. ETFs offer investors the opportunity to buy and sell index fund-type investments, but in real time throughout the trading day rather than only at the close of the market day as with index funds. Investors can also manage taxable events better with ETFs by choosing when (or if) to sell. ETF trades incur brokerage commissions, potentially leading to higher expenses in exchange for this flexibility.

MOVING ON...

Got all those fund types straight? Don't worry, we'll soon introduce you to NAIC's mutual fund analysis tools which will help you make sense of your fund choices before you invest that first penny. But before we get there, let's move on to the mechanics of buying and selling funds.

CHAPTER THIRTEEN

Mutual Fund Mechanics

Introduction

While there are many different types of mutual funds to choose from, they all have some key elements in common. In this chapter we'll introduce *some of these basics, including important fund documentation as well as how to actually buy shares in a mutual fund.*

Mutual fund families

One part of choosing a mutual fund is knowing a little about its fund family. The companies that administer a set of mutual funds are called mutual fund families. Some of the more well-known fund families include Vanguard, Fidelity, T. Rowe Price and Janus. (Remember that these are just examples, not investment recommendations.)

Investors have hundreds of fund families to choose from. Some people prefer to choose funds from only one or two fund families to keep record-keeping more streamlined and simplified. It's also often easier and less costly to transfer money from one fund to another when they're within the same fund family. If you choose a well-respected fund family with a wide variety of funds, keeping all your fund holdings within the same family is certainly a valid option.

Some brokerage and mutual fund accounts allow their customers to buy mutual funds from a wide variety of fund families. For example, if you have an IRA account at Fidelity, you can invest not only in Fidelity funds, but also in funds offered by other mutual fund families. The brokerage/fund family may charge a transaction fee for investing in such "outside" funds, so be sure you investigate this possibility before making your choices.

Keep in mind that you may not have much of a choice in fund families if you're investing through your employer's retirement plan. Some companies offer a wide range of fund options while others might restrict the choices to just a few funds within one fund family. If you're unhappy with the fund options in your employer's plan, be sure to let your company's benefits office know. It's possible that your opinion will influence the company to offer better choices in the future.

Important fund documents

Just as you read over an individual stock's most recent quarterly and annual report (along with other documentation) before investing, it's important that you familiarize yourself with a mutual fund's documentation as well. Be sure to request (and read!) these documents as part of your research before making any investment decisions.

Remember that this book is meant simply as an introduction to stock and mutual fund investing. You'll find more detailed descriptions about these mutual fund documents as well as instructions for interpreting them in the *NAIC Mutual Fund Handbook*.

Prospectus

The mutual fund prospectus functions as an owner's manual of sorts for prospective and current shareholders of that fund. At the very minimum, a prospectus clearly states the fund's goals, strategies, fees, past performance and expenses. Many of the details discussed in the prospectus are fund features we introduced in Chapter 10.

Although no one can force you to read it, the Securities and Exchange Commission (SEC) requires every fund to provide investors with a copy of the fund prospectus either before the first investment or along with the statement confirming an investor's first contribution.

Other Mutual Fund Resources Offered by NAIC

The *NAIC Mutual Fund Handbook* also contains the Bond Fund Check List, Bond Fund Comparison Guide and Bond Fund Trend Report. A description of each tool as well as detailed instructions for using the tools is included.

Additionally, NAIC provides access to all of its mutual fund analysis tools in the Mutual Fund Education and Resource Center on its web site at ***www.better-investing.org/funds.*** Here you also have access to Standard & Poor's mutual fund data and mutual fund reports on over 14,000 stock, bond, international, asset allocation, convertable, moneymarket and exchange traded funds (ETF's). The data is automarically populated into the forms for you so you can get right down to analyzing, comparing, and monitoring funds that best meet your investing needs.

National Association of Investors Corporation

logout | help

JOIN NAIC   Search: [   ] [Go]   START A CLUB

NAIC
ABOUT
MEMBERSHIP
CHAPTERS
CORPORATE MEMBERS
NAIC STORE
SITE SEARCH

MEMBER RESOURCES
MEMBER SERVICE
PUBLICATIONS
COMMUNITY
EDUCATION
CLUBS
YOUTH
SOFTWARE
GREEN SHEETS

PREMIUM SERVICES (OPS)
BITS ONLINE
COMPANY REPORTS

PREMIUM SUBSCRIPTIONS
MUTUAL FUND EDUCATION CENTER
IAS ONLINE

MUTUAL FUND EDUCATION AND RESOURCE CENTER

 **Tool Box**

 **Library**

 **University**

Welcome to the *Better Investing* Mutual Fund Education and Resource Center. Here you will find everything you need to analyze and select mutual funds to meet your investing goals.

In the Tool Box you have access to all of NAIC's mutual fund analysis tools, Standard and Poor's mutual fund data and Standard and Poor's Mutual Fund Reports on over 14,000 mutual funds.

In the Library you will find a number of articles on the subject of stocks, mutual funds and financial planning. NAIC members have full access to all the articles in NAIC's archive and can search the archive by issue, article or author.

The University holds within it a series of 45 lessons providing education on the basics of mutual fund investing. If you're new to the world of mutual fund investing this is the place to begin your journey.

Figure 14-04: NAIC Better Investing Mutual Fund Education and Resource Center

PART FOUR:
Investment Club Basics

e-mail to share their stock research and conduct meetings.

No matter what your situation, regardless of whether or not you're able to meet with other club members in person, you should be able to find or start a club that meets your needs as long as you're willing to put in a solid effort.

Why join?

So what benefits might you hope to gain from an investment club membership? Are clubs really worth the hassle of homework and monthly meetings? That depends on your personality, of course, but we think clubs are an excellent way to stay motivated while improving your investment know-how.

Most successful investment clubs exhibit a combination of these three main elements:

Education

At the heart of the club experience is an opportunity for ongoing investment education. The most successful investment clubs have a formal, well-defined

It's not even necessary for club members to live in close proximity to each other for their club to be a success. Clubs with members spread far and wide geographically may get together only once every two or three months but then hold a much longer meeting. Some clubs never meet face to face at all, conducting all their communication and club business online with computers by using club Web sites and

education curriculum designed by the members as a group to educate themselves on the financial topics they're most interested in mastering.

Many clubs even elect an education officer, whose main responsibility is to organize and present some sort of educational lesson at each meeting, ensuring that the club members are constantly expanding their investment knowledge.

Companionship

Of course you can learn almost anything you'd need to know about investing in the comfort and privacy of your home with the help of books and online materials. But why do all the work yourself when you can share the load, as well as the knowledge, with people whose company you enjoy?

When investment clubs work well, it's because the members pool their intellectual resources and curiosity to learn more with less effort than they could on their own. If you like the camaraderie of working in a group that has a shared purpose or if you feel a little insecure about learning a whole new subject on your own, a club could be a great place to start your investment education because of the shared responsibility and social interaction.

Shared investments

Most investment clubs pool their investment funds into a shared portfolio, regularly contributing $30 or $40 or $50 a month and then investing those funds in stocks they judge to have the most potential for positive growth. Lots of people investing relatively small amounts of money means it's possible to invest a larger sum of money in each chosen stock, minimizing the percentage of the investment that goes towards paying brokerage expenses.

If you don't have much money to invest but are too impatient to wait until you have more, investment clubs offer an efficient way to start building your portfolio now. You would be hard-pressed to find a way to invest a sum as relatively small as $25 in individual stocks on your own without paying an oppressive percentage of that on brokerage commissions. In a club with 10 or 15 members, your share of the commission would be just a fraction of what you would pay if you were investing on your own.

Not a joiner?

Investment clubs aren't the right choice for everyone, of course. If it would frustrate you to have to rely on other people who might not work as hard as you do, or if you prefer to make your own investing decisions instead of discussing them with a host of potentially contrary club members, you're probably better off investing on your own. Clubs with inactive members who don't pull their own weight or with ill-defined objectives that get in the way of efficient club operations can be a nightmare for even the most dedicated individual. Schedule conflicts can also make meeting times inconvenient.

Assess your own personality and your level of attraction to the idea of throwing yourself into a club before you actually make the leap. Take some time to investigate potential clubs, screening them thoroughly before deciding to join them. (You'll find questions to ask in Chapter 16.) Know what you're looking for, and what you're not. Once you've done your homework, you can simply say "no thanks" if you decide the club scene isn't right for you.

Self-directed investment clubs

If you like the idea of learning to invest in the company of other people but are either wary of commingling your money with theirs or simply can't invest in a club account for whatever reason, there's another opportunity for you to have a satisfying club experience. *Self-directed investment (SDI) clubs* still provide investors with the typical club experience of meeting regularly in pursuit of investment education and stock analysis. The difference is that after the club agrees on any investment decisions, club members invest

through their own personal accounts and not through a shared club account. Since SDI club members never pool their money, there's no need for them to form under a legal structure such as a partnership.

Because SDI clubs have no regular monthly contributions and no checking or brokerage accounts, there's also no need for a club treasurer, club accounting software or annual tax filings. SDI club enthusiasts find this can lead to more efficient club meetings because they can focus entirely on the education and social aspects of the club while ignoring the sometimes-tedious accounting tasks.

The SDI club framework is well suited for online clubs where the members never meet face to face and sometimes will never meet each other in person. It can be time-consuming or complicated for online clubs to collect member signatures on *partnership agreements* or brokerage account applications, for instance. SDI clubs don't have the same paperwork needs as more traditional clubs, so this kind of effort is rarely necessary.

While an SDI club may not have a legal partnership agreement, the members will still want to create by-laws and a club investment philosophy to ensure that they all understand their club responsibilities. You'll learn more about the importance of these club documents in later chapters.

One of the few drawbacks of SDI clubs over clubs with pooled assets is that at times, some members may not take their club responsibilities as seriously because they have no money invested in the club. Dealing with this lack of motivation on the part of a few club members can lead to frustration and discord for the club as a whole.

This is one reason why it's especially important for SDI clubs to create detailed club operating procedures with explicit consequences for members who don't live up to their responsibilities, and to thoroughly screen members before allowing them to join to make sure they understand the commitment they're making when they join.

A little history

The earliest known American investment clubs began in the 1880's. Today there are over 28,000 clubs registered with NAIC. The average investment club consists of 11 members investing $84 monthly, with a club portfolio of over $63,000. It's estimated that several million American investors have been part of an investment club at one time or another.

Investment clubs like the Mutual Investment Club of Detroit gave soldiers stationed abroad during World War II the opportunity to invest part of their earnings even though they were out of the country and couldn't attend to the investing themselves during that time. Military clubs still exist today, though the club members can often be much more involved in day-to-day club activities thanks to online communication.

Investment clubs are found all over the United States and are known to be in over twenty other countries around the world as well. Club members range in age from young infants whose parents invest for them in a family club to older retirees working to make the most of their savings.

The Beardstown Ladies

Probably the most well-known investment club of the last decade or so is the Beardstown Ladies' Investment Club of Beardstown, Illinois. Ask anyone who formed an investment club in the mid 1990s where they found their initial inspiration and a fair number will undoubtedly point to one of the Beardstown Ladies' books or media appearances as a prominent influence. With their humble, homespun style

and their Wall Street smarts, the Ladies gave hope to small investors everywhere that they, too, could learn to invest by forming an investment club.

Unfortunately, the Beardstown Ladies' overwhelmingly positive influence on investors was marred a bit in 1998 when they discovered that they'd inadvertently overstated their club returns due to data entry mistakes in the club accounting software. While this simple error was definitely a serious matter for a club presenting itself as an investment club authority, newspapers and other financial media sources publicized it as a reason to be wary of investing in individual stocks. The news stories often focused on the

Beardstown Ladies' mistake as evidence that investment clubs, or even investing directly in stocks at all, were too complicated and risky for the investors.

There's no way of knowing how many investors were discouraged from starting or joining an investment club by these media reports. Regardless of the investment returns of any one club, famous or not, clubs still offer a unique and valuable opportunity for investors looking to expand their financial knowledge.

Joining an Investment Club

Introduction

You've decided that you would like to be part of an investment club, but you can't or don't want to start a club of your own. What now? Sounds like it's time to find a club looking for new members!

Looking for a club

It's not as easy as you might think to find an investment club looking for new members in your area. The most optimistic scenario is that a club you're already aware of approaches you and asks you to join. But if the local clubs you know about don't have any openings or if you've never even heard of any clubs operating nearby (the most likely case), where do you turn next?

Investment clubs are discouraged from advertising for new members by Securities and Exchange Commission (SEC) rules that might be interpreted to mean that in some situations clubs could be classified as mutual funds rather than investment clubs. Since this could prove to be a costly and unwelcome consequence of advertising for new members, most clubs choose to take a more discreet route when searching out new members.

One of the best ways to find clubs looking for new members is to become involved with your local NAIC chapter. Most chapters offer regular educational classes and larger investment events, and often a more social networking time where you might find clubs open to new members. Attending these events or even becoming a chapter volunteer will give you the best possible opportunity to learn about club openings.

The same SEC rules mentioned above unfortunately prevent NAIC and its chapters from directly matching up clubs with potential members. To offer an alternative method of matchmaking, many chapters will instead put up sheets of

paper on bulletin boards or in notebooks where clubs looking for members and members looking for clubs can post contact information.

Chapters might also ask for a representative from clubs looking for members to stand up at the beginning of an event so that members looking for clubs can identify someone to look for when the event is over. While these methods of getting clubs and members together might seem a bit clandestine, they're the best alternative currently available due to liability and other reasons.

If there are community bulletin boards in your area, at the supermarket or library, for example, you may want to post an ad that you're looking for an already established investment club. Community newsletters, such as for a church or social group, can serve the same purpose.

If this approach leads to contact from a local club, please be careful to screen this club even more thoroughly than you would a club you encounter at an NAIC event to ensure that it fits your investment philosophy and educational needs. Not every investment club follows NAIC stock selection guidelines

or is even a member of NAIC at all. Be sure that you understand a club's operating procedures and investment philosophy before you join.

If you've spent a lot of time and effort looking for a club to join but have come up empty-handed, you'll probably want to consider starting a club of your own. While a new club can be a little time-consuming in the first few months, there's a lot to be said for knowing that you'll be creating exactly the type of club you want. You can learn a little more about the basics for starting a club from scratch in Chapter 17.

What to look for in an investment club

Once you've finally found a promising club (or two, perhaps) that's looking for new members, your work has only just begun. Now you need to evaluate whether the club you've located is the right club for you. Don't even think of joining a club until you've attended at least three meetings, talked to at least one member in depth and looked for the key club elements listed below.

If a club isn't willing to let you sit in on their meetings or to show you their most basic club documents, that's not the club you want to throw your hard-earned money into. Organized and well-run clubs will be very enthusiastic about giving you the information you need to conduct a thorough screening and probably run you through a screening of their own as well. A club may not be willing to show a casual prospective member their member valuation statements (how much each member's investment in the club is worth) due to privacy concerns. They should, however, show you the entire club's valuation, including which stocks they hold in their portfolio.

Formal structure

Any club you consider joining should have formal written documents detailing the club's structure and operating procedures. At minimum, the club should share with you its legal partnership agreement (assuming the club is structured as a partnership, as the majority of clubs are) and its *club operating procedures* (sometimes called *bylaws*). Read through the partnership agreement to ensure that there's nothing you object to, but give the club operating procedures more of your attention. The partnership agreement is rarely updated and is usually only changed when partners are added to or removed from the club.

The club operating procedures, on the other hand, are the living documentation of club operations and should be reviewed and updated as needed at least once a year. These are just a few of the items the club operating procedures should set forth:

CLUB OPERATING PROCEDURES

- when, where and how often the club meets
- the minimum monthly member contribution
- where the club's investment accounts are held
- when the club's valuation statement (an accounting of the club's portfolio) is updated
- the types of officers the club has (as well as officer duties)
- fines or penalties the club assesses for late or missed contributions and unexcused meeting absences.

The club operating procedures should also explain membership issues such as admitting new members, withdrawing outgoing members and a listing of the expectations and responsibilities of all members.

Investment philosophy

Look for information in the club operating procedures about how the club researches stocks, including how often each member is required to present a stock to the entire club, and whether the club breaks up into smaller groups to analyze stocks. If you don't find this information in the operating procedures, be sure to ask the club what is expected of members in terms of stock research and education responsibilities.

One of the most important parts of the club operating procedures is the club's investment philosophy. This should explain the club's approach towards its investments, whether it believes in a short or long-term outlook and whether it analyzes potential stocks using a fundamental or technical framework. (Turn to Chapter 6 if you need a refresher on any of these terms).

If the club doesn't include its investment philosophy in any of its documents, be sure to ask about it at one of the meetings you observe. If the club has

never actually decided on an investment philosophy, your questions may spur it to do so. If you can't get an answer to this basic question, though, or if you get conflicting answers, think hard before joining this club. You may later find yourself owning stocks you wouldn't buy on your own if the club's philosophy doesn't mesh with yours.

Club history

If possible, find out a little about the club's history. How long ago was it created, and how many of the original members are still in the club? How many new members have been admitted, and how many members have withdrawn? If a club you're interested in has a high member turnover rate, this may be a warning sign of a poorly run club.

Watch out for...

Other warning signs include members who rarely do stock or other educational presentations, as well as members who don't bother showing up at club meetings or making their monthly financial contributions at all. By looking over the partnership agreement and club operating procedures, you should be able to spot a club with poorly defined objectives. And if the club doesn't have written club operating procedures at all...say so long and keep looking for something better!

These are just a few of the things you'll want to look for before you consider joining an already established club. You'll find much more detail about evaluating a potential club in the *NAIC Investment Club Operations Handbook*.

Starting an Investment Club

Introduction

If you can't find a local investment club that's looking for new members or you just don't like the clubs you've seen, it's time to consider starting a club of your own. You might also prefer to start a club rather than join an existing club if you have very specific ideas for how your club should operate.

Important club resources

Starting an investment club can be time consuming, but it can also be highly rewarding. It's easiest to start a club when you have good resources to turn to for help. In addition to what you'll find in this chapter, you'll want to read the *NAIC Investment Club Operations Handbook*, another title in the *Better Investing* educational series, and one that's devoted solely to starting, joining and running successful investment clubs.

You can also find a great deal of help at the NAIC Web Site and through your local NAIC chapter, which may offer classes on starting and running clubs. Attending classes through your local chapter is a great way to meet members from established clubs who will probably be more than willing to offer advice or assistance as you start your own club.

The first steps

Once you know you'd like to start a club, your next few steps are very clear, though not always so easy. Remember to be deliberate, take your time and focus on exactly the type of club to create as you begin organizing. At the very least, read through the investment club chapters in this book once or twice before attempting to explain the investment club concept to anyone else. Better yet, read through the *NAIC Investment Club Operations Handbook* since it contains much more detail than these merely introductory chapters. Once you're feeling comfortable enough to answer questions from potential club members, it's time to get started!

Finding prospective members

If you're going to have a successful investment club, you're going to need at least a few other people beside yourself to join up. A good rule of thumb is to invite at least twice as many people to your introductory meeting as you hope will actually join the club.

Some people may seem very interested when you first describe the investment club concept but then change their mind after they hear about the level of commitment required to be a club member. This is okay—you only want the most dedicated people to actually join your club. It's better to clear out the wishy-washy types before the club even forms.

Aim for a good mix of personalities within the club when at all possible. If you have too many assertive leaders, for example, they may spend the entire meeting trying to wrestle control from each other. Too many quiet, passive members, though, and decisions will never get made. Of course you won't be able to foresee every potential personality clash, so just try not to invite any currently feuding neighbors or other obvious unlikely pairings to your introductory meeting.

So where should you go to find potential club members? You may want to stick very close to home and invite members of your family or some close friends. Expand your circle a little and consider co-workers, neighbors and fellow members of religious organizations and any social clubs you belong to. Don't forget to attend events given by your local NAIC chapter

and let any participants there know that you'll soon be starting a new club.

Make sure that everyone you talk to understands that this is just an introductory meeting. They're under no obligation to join the club or even to come to another meeting. Reinforce to them that they'll have time to think things over before they're asked to make a commitment. This initial meeting is just to explain and discuss the philosophy, operations and goals of an investment club.

Ask people who have accepted your invitation to bring an interested friend or two along with them to the meeting. It may turn out that the original prospect bows out but that their friend becomes the club's most dedicated member!

Your first meeting—introducing the concept

Once you've got a group of people interested, find a meeting place that will comfortably hold them all and publicize the meeting date, time and location. If it's a small group (or you've got an exceptionally large living room), you may want to hold this first meeting at your house. Other options include a meeting room at a local school or library, or maybe a room one of the other attendees has access to through work or other connections. If at all possible, find a room with little or no rental charge.

Half an hour before the meeting, you should be ready for your invited guests. While refreshments would most likely be welcome and help to put people at ease, they certainly aren't required. You should bring some sort of written explanation of what, exactly, an investment club is. Having a handout that people can look over later at home may help answer any questions they still have. Make some NAIC brochures and membership catalogs, which discuss NAIC resources such as books, software and classes, available as well. You can obtain NAIC materials from your local chapter or by calling NAIC toll free at (877) ASK NAIC.

Nametags are essential at this first meeting unless everyone you've invited already knows everyone else. You should also create and copy an agenda for the evening so everyone at the meeting has a clear idea of what's going to happen.

The agenda doesn't need to be long or involved. The key elements are introductions around the room, an explanation of the investment club concept and a description of a typical club member's responsibilities and time commitment. Explain that the first year will most likely require a higher time commitment than later years, simply because the club needs to be created from scratch. New club members may also need to devote additional time to education as they learn more about analyzing stocks.

Let your meeting guests know that they can expect to spend at least four or five hours a month on club activities outside of the monthly meeting. Assure them that these hours should lessen after the first year, when all the basics have been dealt with and the education program begins to be balanced by stock presentations.

After all these explanations, answer any questions that people may have. Once the questions are done, it's time to take the biggest step of all and ask a question of your own. This is the time for people to decide if they'd like to proceed. If enough people say yes, set a time and place for your next meeting and collect contact information from everyone who expressed an interest.

Let the people who show interest know that the next meeting will be packed with business so they should come prepared for some serious work and decision-making. Also tell them to bring their checkbooks, since the monthly contribution amount will be decided upon and then collected at the very next meeting.

Your second meeting—making things official

While attendance may be a lot lower at your new club's second meeting, never fear. There's a much greater chance that the people who came back for this meeting are actually interested in making the club a successful reality. After a brief bit of some more "getting to know you" chitchat if necessary, move right into the critical business at hand. There's a lot to be discussed and decided at this second meeting, most importantly creating the formal club structure.

1 Club name

A nice way to break the ice at your second meeting is to brainstorm and then select a name for your club. Have fun with this— tap your creativity and see what you all come up with. You might want your name to reference something you all have in common or your geographical location or choose something investment related. The actual name doesn't matter as much as

all your members being comfortable and happy with it.

2 Monthly contribution

This is another fairly quick decision you can make near the beginning of the meeting that will help you and your new club members feel like part of a real group. Decide how much your monthly contribution will be, and then if members are allowed to contribute more than that amount. Some clubs will set a minimum monthly contribution of $25, for example, and also permit members to

contribute more if desired. Allowing larger contributions helps your club accumulate money to invest in the stocks of your choice much more quickly.

Club accounting software makes dealing with unequal member contributions a breeze, so don't worry about trying to keep every member's piece of the club equal. You may want to set a cap for any one member's club ownership to avoid one member potentially dominating club decision-making. You'll find more discussion of this issue in the *NAIC Investment Club Operations Handbook.*

Once you've come to an agreement on the monthly contribution amount and elected a treasurer (we'll get to that a bit later), everyone should write out a check for their first club contribution. Whoever is elected as treasurer will have to hold onto the checks until a bank or brokerage account is opened in the club's name, but it's still important symbolically to gather member contributions even at this early point.

You may also decide to collect an additional sum of money for start-up costs at the next or a later meeting to cover software or other expenses, but these funds are on top of regular monthly contributions. Again, you'll find much more detail about these issues in the *NAIC Investment Club Operations Handbook*.

❸ Partnership Agreement

Once you have an official name, it's time to decide on an official structure. Most investment clubs choose to form as a legal partnership. NAIC's sample partnership agreement, included in the appendix of this book and also found online at NAIC's Web Site, offers a strong legal document that your club can freely modify or even copy outright. You are encouraged to consult with your own legal and tax advisors.

Read through the document *thoroughly* before deciding if every part of it is right for your club, and make any necessary changes, after consulting your attorney. Some clubs will adopt the sample partnership agreement with very limited changes with the understanding that any member can propose changes after a few months, which will

then be discussed and voted on by the club as a whole.

❹ Club operating procedures

The partnership agreement sets your club's legal status, but the clubs operating procedures (referred to as bylaws by some clubs) are the real rules your club lives by. The club operating procedures detail such important guidelines as your club's investment philosophy, meeting time and place, monthly financial contribution, educational objectives, new member and withdrawing member issues, and many more.

You'll find a sample set of club operating procedures

in the *NAIC Investment Club Operations Handbook*. As with the sample partnership agreement, your club could adopt these sample club operating procedures as your own with appropriate changes, then revisit the entire document to make whatever other changes are necessary after a few months of actual club experience.

Unlike the partnership agreement, you can expect your club operating procedures to change on a somewhat regular basis as your club grows and evolves. You may find that some club policies you earlier agreed to in theory just don't work in practice, or that you need some formal addition to the club operating procedures regarding an issue you'd never even considered until it came up in the course of day-to-day club operation.

You should formally review your club operating procedures together as a club at least once a year, making any adjustments necessary, as part of your annual club maintenance. You'll find more information on this procedure and other yearly club tasks in Chapter 18.

5 **Officer elections**

One of the decisions you'll need to make when writing your club operating procedures is the number and type of club officer positions to create. Once they're set, it's time for a few of your club members to step up to the plate and take responsibility. Officer elections are crucial at this meeting. At the very least you'll need a President/Presiding Partner to lead the meetings and make work assignments, and a Treasurer/Financial Partner to find and open a brokerage account and start to learn the accounting ropes. A Vice-President and Education Officer are also very important.

6 **Brokerage account**

Choosing a brokerage firm need not be an overwhelming task for club members. The *NAIC Investment Club Operations Handbook,* as well as portions of Chapter 9, will give you more guidance on this important decision. Many investment clubs choose a discount broker with its lower commissions. They don't see any reason to incur the higher expenses charged by a full-service broker when they won't need that broker's investment recommendations. Some clubs prefer guidance from full-service brokers when the club is new to the investment process. Your club will need to make this decision for itself, of course.

7 **Computer/software decisions**

Another choice your club will need to make right away is the extent to which you'll be using computers and online resources. There are clubs that take care of all club business by hand and in person, and clubs that do everything, even conduct meetings, online with their computers. Depending on your club members' access to computers and comfort level using software and online resources, your club may find these resources either impossible to function without or nice but hardly necessary.

Computers and online resources can make some essential club business, especially club accounting, a snap. Spending less time on the busywork means more club time for the good stuff— education, stock analysis and enjoying each other's company. Even if some of your club members don't have computers, you should still strongly consider using, at the very least, club accounting software to make your treasurer's job easier.

Otherwise, most club business can be taken care of either by hand or with a computer. For example, your club can use either the paper or software versions of NAIC's stock analysis tools such as the Stock Selection Guide (SSG). Some members may have a strong preference to do their research with pencil and paper while others would find the extra work involved to be a waste of time when data can be

129

downloaded, using NAIC OPS data (described below), for example, into their software in an instant instead of keyed in by hand.

As long as your club discusses this issue and comes to an acceptable consensus, how much or how little you all end up using computers doesn't really matter. But it's a safe bet to say that once you explore the computerized and online resources available, you'll have little motivation to go back to doing things "the old-fashioned way." You'll find more explanation of these resources in Chapter 19, and a full description and instructions for using them in the *NAIC Computerized Investing & the Internet Handbook*.

8 NAIC membership

One last bit of essential club business should be collecting dues for NAIC membership. We've already covered many of the benefits of NAIC membership in Part I. The main benefits of membership for your club are the monthly issues of *Better Investing* magazine, critical club accounting information, access to software for club accounting and stock analysis, and the support from local NAIC chapter volunteers. Members also receive discounts on software as well as registration costs for national and many regional events.

Club members can also choose to purchase an optional annual subscription to Online Premium Services (OPS), which gives access to continually updated data to be downloaded into stock analysis and stock screening software. (You can read more about this tremendous membership benefit in Chapter 19.)

The sooner your club joins NAIC, the sooner you'll have access to a wide range of educational resources and the sooner you'll begin to receive *Better Investing*. Once your membership

dues are submitted, your club's designated representative (usually the president or presiding partner) will also be notified of educational classes and events offered by your local NAIC chapter.

Your third meeting and beyond—continuing the journey

Once your club officers have been elected, your meeting time and place set, your partnership agreement signed and submitted (according to your state and county's requirements), your club operating procedures ratified and your brokerage account opened, you're done with the more tedious, bureaucratic aspects of getting your club started. Now you can start to follow a more traditional meeting structure and get down to the business of actually running the club and learning about investing.

There's still a lot of planning and decision-making ahead of your club, but the bulk of the organizational paperwork is behind you now. The next chapter will detail some of the elements of a typical club meeting and help you construct a long-term vision for your club's operations.

Meet an NAIC Investment Club

The Super Investors Club of Apache Junction

Most investment clubs are the traditional type, gathering month after month in some meeting room or at a member's home, discussing stock analysis and financial education in a fairly routine manner. There's nothing wrong with this way of doing business, of course, but the twenty members of the Super Investors Club of Apache Junction, Arizona prefer to follow a less traditional road. Following the road is something these women all have in common. While the Super Investors meet regularly in person over the winter months, they head their separate ways each summer to explore new roads in their RVs.

Six months of the year, these adventurous retirees meet every Tuesday afternoon in an RV park in the Superstition Mountains of Arizona where they all spend the winter. Like more traditional clubs, they use NAIC's Stock Selection Guide to study stocks together, purchasing the ones that meet their standards. But they also hit the road for field trips to visit companies they're interested in, or to attend the annual shareholder meetings of the companies they own whenever possible.

Many members of the Super Investors use NAIC Classic software, and the other members are expecting to use their computers to streamline the stock research process in the future, as well. The club also takes advantage of online club accounting resources so that every member can stay up to date regardless of where they might be geographically. They don't hold formal meetings over the summer months, but they do stay in touch through e-mail. They plan to begin exchanging SSGs online so they can continue their investment research together no matter how far apart they may be on the map.

With a typical waiting list of at least six women eager to join the club, the current members frequently debate whether or not to increase the size of the club. It's clear that their dedication and creative club operating procedures have combined to make this one club well worth traveling to join.

Running an Investment Club

Introduction

Your investment club structure is set and you've made a lot of important decisions. Now the real fun begins! This chapter will lead you through the basics *of establishing the monthly and annual procedures necessary for your club's long-term success.*

Your investment club's third meeting represents a fundamental shift in focus and in practice. It's time to settle into a more traditional structure for your monthly meetings, a structure that follows a regular agenda and includes the same basic elements month after month.

This chapter is intended only as a very basic overview of the types of issues your new club might encounter during your first year of operation as you start to establish a meeting routine. You'll find much more detailed guidance on club operations and accounting matters in two other books in the Better Investing educational series, the *NAIC Investment Club Operations Handbook* and the *NAIC Club Accounting Handbook*.

For the first year or so, you and your fellow club members may find yourselves, every now and then, still dealing with business relating to starting up a new club. Fit these tasks into the "new business" section of your agenda, and then deal with them at the next regularly scheduled meeting.

Creating your monthly meeting agenda

Your third meeting, really the first "official" club meeting with your new officers and procedures, should be formal and well organized. Your club's president or presiding officer should set the agenda in advance of the meeting, even distributing it by e-mail a few days before if your club uses computers to facilitate communication. Here's an example of items found on a typical investment club's agenda.

SAMPLE MEETING AGENDA ITEMS

1. Call meeting to order
2. Approve meeting minutes
3. Collect member contributions
4. Distribute valuation statements
5. Treasurer's report
6. Portfolio/stock watcher reports
7. New stock presentation(s)
8. Stock buy and sell discussions
9. Educational presentation
10. Unfinished business
11. New business
12. Homework for next meeting

Establishing your education program

Once your club comes up with an agenda to follow for your monthly meetings, it's time to focus on your investment education. You'll want to get started planning your club's education program as soon as your third meeting because there's a lot to be learned. NAIC's books, tools and online resources are a logical place to start.

If most or all of your club members are investing novices, you should start by thoroughly reviewing this book, which is meant as an introduction to many aspects of investing in stocks and mutual funds. Once you're all comfortable with the basic concepts, you should continue your educational journey by focusing more exclusively on stock analysis.

The best place to learn more about NAIC's stock selection philosophy and tools is in the *NAIC Stock Selection Handbook*. One strategy you might choose is for every club member to read a chapter each month between meetings, and then to devote 15 or 20 minutes of each club meeting to a discussion of what you've read.

Your entire club can also attend classes offered by your local NAIC chapter, or pay for a few members to attend and then bring back what they learn to share with the rest of the club. As you start to learn to complete first the Stock Check List and then the Stock Selection Guide, both covered in detail in the *NAIC Stock Selection Handbook*, local classes and online resources can help make the process even easier.

You'll find many more ideas for creating and implementing your club's education program in the *NAIC Investment Club Operations Handbook*. One section of that book is dedicated to educational lessons and exercises for club members. There are 24 lessons, with exercises, for your club members to learn the basics about investing. If you use these educational sessions monthly, you will have enough lessons for two full years!

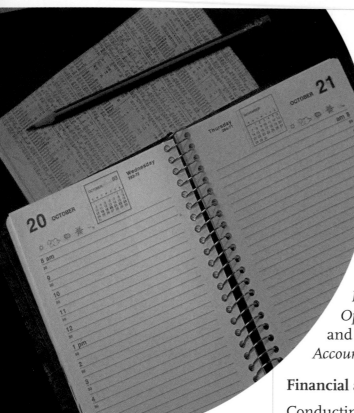

Creating a calendar of annual tasks

In addition to setting a monthly to-do list (your meeting agenda), your club should also make a schedule for completing other less frequent, but still important, club business items. There are certain items of club business, such as taxes and an annual audit, which must be dealt with every year. Knowing in advance what is required and when each task will be accomplished will help your club stay organized and ahead of the game.

Here are a few of the club business items you can expect to encounter year after year. Remember that this list is just an overview. You can find much more information about when and how to complete each of these tasks in the *NAIC Investment Club Operations Handbook* and the *NAIC Club Accounting Handbook*.

Financial audit

Conducting an annual audit of all of your club's financial transactions is one of the most critical tasks a club should do, and also one that many clubs frequently neglect. The audit should only take a few hours for your club's audit committee to complete, but will give your entire club peace of mind that your records are accurate and up to date. Step by step instructions for completing the audit can be found at the NAIC Web Site.

NAIC membership renewal

Take a few minutes to collect NAIC renewal checks from your club members each year so that you'll continue to reap the benefits of membership.

Club operating procedures review

Spend 20 minutes or so at one club meeting a year to read your club operating procedures out loud. Make any adjustments or additions necessary to accurately reflect your club's ongoing operations.

Tax form preparation and filing

There are lots of fantastic reasons for your club's treasurer to use club accounting software and online resources, but probably the biggest is how much more quickly and accurately your annual tax forms can be prepared with a computer than by hand. While the software will produce your club's tax forms, you are encouraged to also seek a tax professional for any questions or concerns.

Portfolio review

Your club should also review all of your portfolio holdings in detail at least once a year. Portfolio management and review gives your club a way to assess your stock selection technique, to evaluate whether or not you're sticking to your club's stated investment philosophy. You can find more information about this process in the *NAIC Using Portfolio Management Wisdom Handbook*.

Education curriculum

Even after you've learned to analyze individual stocks, there are still years worth of educational topics you can investigate together through regular educational segments at your monthly meetings. Once a year, take a survey to find out what financial topics your club members are most interested in exploring next. Then create an education curriculum for the upcoming year that will cover the most popular subjects.

Tips for club success

As you and your club members become more comfortable with the month to month operation of your club and with your newly expanding investment knowledge, you may have a tendency to relax a little and let things coast for awhile. You should certainly congratulate yourselves for creating a successful, supportive club environment, but this is probably the time to work even harder to ensure that your success continues on.

Clubs that stay successful over the long-term share a certain set of characteristics and habits. Your club should consider making most, if not all, of these elements a priority if you intend to thrive for more than a year or two. Remember, this is just a listing of items to consider. For more details on ways to keep your members motivated and your club successful, look to the *NAIC Investment Club Operations Handbook.*

Other investment club resources

In addition to the investment club resources that NAIC offers, you can find valuable information on starting and running your club at the Web sites listed in the Online Resource Guide at the end of this book. This is just a sampling of online investing resources. For a more complete list of online and computerized resources, consult the *NAIC Computerized Investing & the Internet Handbook.*

REMEMBER THESE KEY ACTIONS:

- *Focus on continuing education*

- *Choose new members carefully*

- *Mentor new members after they join*

- *Assess your club's portfolio at least once a year*

- *Follow the spirit and letter of your club operating procedures*

- *Take advantage of investment resources, both locally and online*

- *Use computers to reduce your club's workload*

PART FIVE:
Beyond the Basics

Turning to Your Computer

Introduction

Whether you're a complete computer novice or addicted to the Internet, computer software and online resources can simplify your investment research tasks and save you much time and effort. NAIC offers a variety of software products and online education resources to help investors with

mutual fund and stock analysis, portfolio management and investment club accounting.

You'll find more details about these resources in the NAIC Computerized Investing & the Internet Handbook, so here's a brief overview for now.

NAIC's Web Site

Your first investing stop after you open your Web browser should be NAIC's Web Site. You'll find plenty of educational resources, as well as guidance on stock selection and starting and running a successful investment club.

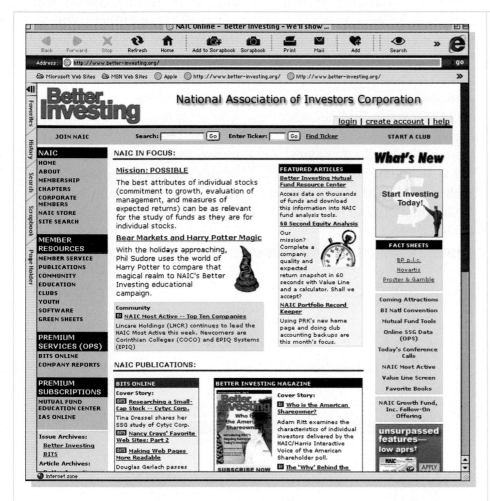

Figure 19-01: NAIC's home page

Community

One of the most unique and supportive aspects of NAIC's Web Site is the potential to meet other investors with a similar philosophy, regardless of where you live or whether or not you have a regional NAIC chapter close by. Through e-mail and Web interaction, you can join the thousands of NAIC investors who have already found a supportive investing community online where they can ask questions and learn from their peers.

In addition to the educational aspect of these online communities, many NAIC members have made deep, long-lasting friendships with fellow members, friendships that have thrived for years online, regardless of whether or not the friends will ever meet in person. That's just further testimony to the power of NAIC's education programs and investment philosophy, as well as to its volunteer-based structure that changes investors' lives for the better.

I-Club-List

The largest community of NAIC members online can be found on *NAIC's I-Club-List*, a free e-mail-based discussion list with a current roster of more than 3,000 members. Created and run as a true labor of love by dedicated volunteers, the I-Club-List has been offering investors a safe environment to ask questions and share investment knowledge since 1995.

I-Club-List subscribers receive messages daily through e-mail or by visiting the list's Web site where messages can also be read. Topics posted to the I-Club-List range from basic questions about completing the SSG to advanced discussions of cash flow or predicting earnings growth. Regardless of the topics, investors of any level of expertise can find something new each day to increase their knowledge, and are always free to ask whatever questions they may have.

Subscribers can also search the I-Club-List archives for guidance on many topics. Past educational workshops stretching over a period of days on the I-Club-List have been archived at the NAIC Web Site as well, offering timeless lessons on a variety of subjects. NAIC members can subscribe to the I-Club-List or any of NAIC's other free e-mail lists by going online to NAIC's Web Site and clicking on the "Community" link.

Club Treasurers List

NAIC's Club Treasurers List is another e-mail-based educational list, but devoted to helping investment club treasurers answer their most pressing and difficult questions. The Club Treasurers List is monitored by the creators of NAIC's club accounting software and online accounting tools, as well as by a variety of tax professionals and experienced club treasurers who willingly volunteer their knowledge to help their fellow NAIC members when they need it most.

You can find the Club Treasurers List online at NAIC's Web Site (click on the "Community" link).

NAIC regional chapter lists

Many of NAIC's regional chapters host e-mail-based discussion or announcement lists as well. Some lists are much more active than others, but all offer NAIC members a way to keep in touch with local educational offerings and other events. You can find out what e-mail lists and other online resources your local chapter has available by visiting its Web site. The list of all regional NAIC chapters can be found at NAIC's Web Site.

Special interest lists

When you're not in the mood for in-depth investment discussion but still want some contact with fellow NAIC members, you might try out the NAIC Chat List. As the list guidelines state, this list is for idle chatter only, or "nothing serious, please!" Conversations that go far off-topic on the I-Club-List are commonly redirected to the Chat List, where members can indulge their desire for non-investment discussions.

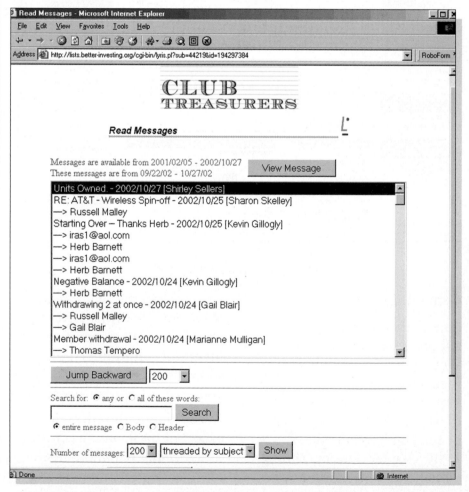

Figure 19-02: Sample view of NAIC's Club Treasurers List online

Speaking of fun conversations, there's also a list for NAIC members planning to attend CompuFest, one of NAIC's annual national events. Many I-Club-List members make the annual trip to CompuFest, and use the CompuFest e-mail list to discuss such subjects as registration, the host city, seminar topics and instructors and where to meet up after hours. *Better Investing* National Convention attendees have their own e-mail list as well.

Even if you're not planning to go to either of these events, you're more than welcome to join the lists (and the conversation). Visit these two lists online at NAIC's Web Site (click on the "Community" link).

NAIC Forum on CompuServe

One other online home for NAIC members exists at the NAIC Forum on CompuServe, where a dedicated group of members congregate to discuss a variety of investment ideas. Volunteers created the NAIC Forum on CompuServe in 1986, in the early days of the Internet, as a way for NAIC members to communicate with each other online regardless of how far apart they lived geographically.

The Forum hosts educational workshops on its message

boards, many of which you can find archived in the Forum's online library. You can also find examples of club partnership agreements and club operating procedures in the libraries, as well as data files, spreadsheets and stock analyses that NAIC members may find useful.

The message sections consist of more than a dozen separate topic areas where Forum members can ask for help or share investment research. Online discussions can focus on a particular stock or element of portfolio management or be as broad as a debate of the concept of diversification in general.

Other investing discussions, including the monthly meeting of NAIC's online investment club called the Challenge Club, take place in one of the NAIC Forums on CompuServe's three conference rooms. Transcripts of some of these events can be found in the file libraries, and minutes from the Challenge Club meetings are frequently posted to the I-Club-List for further discussion.

Investors of any level are welcome to participate in the NAIC Forum on CompuServe. Some of NAIC's most dedicated and knowledgeable volunteers were once brand-new investors whose discovery of the NAIC Forum on CompuServe led to educational opportunities they never realized existed online. In fact, the world's first online investment club, the Pioneers On-Line Investment Club (POLIC), was founded in 1991 by Forum members and made its first online home there.

CompuServe Forum membership is free and requires only a

simple registration process. You can find more information about and specific directions to the NAIC Forum on CompuServe at NAIC's Web Site. You can also find the Forum's Web site URL in the Online Resource Guide at the end of this book.

Education

Among the educational items you'll find at NAIC's Web Site are transcripts of two years worth of classes from NAIC's *Online Investors School* as well as numerous workshops that were originally presented on the I-Club-List. The Investors School offered weekly online educational events ranging from a discussion of *Better Investing* magazine's monthly Stock to Study, a monthly meeting of the online investment club prototype called the Challenge Club (which now meets at the NAIC Forum on CompuServe), industry studies, book discussions and portfolio management classes, to name just a few.

The Investors School was created and produced by a dedicated group of volunteers spread across the United States. Although the Investors School is no longer in operation, transcripts from almost every educational event are still available at NAIC's Web Site (click on the "Education" link).

Better Investing archives

One of the deepest educational resources at the NAIC Web Site is the archive of hundreds of articles from past issues of *Better Investing* magazine available to NAIC members. You can also find archives of BITS, the publication of NAIC's Computer Group Advisory Board (now published exclusively online). By searching these archives, you'll have access to a treasure trove of information on stock analysis, portfolio management, investment club operations, mutual fund education and a multitude of other topics.

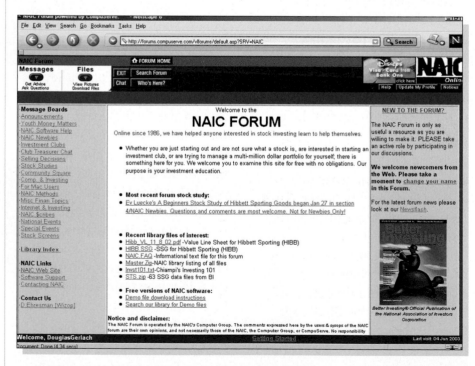

Figure 19-03: Sample view of the NAIC Forum on CompuServe

Low Cost Investment Plan

You'll also find information about NAIC's Low Cost Investment Plan at the NAIC Web Site. This service allows NAIC members to inexpensively purchase the first share of stock often required to participate in corporate dividend reinvestment plans (DRIPs). You can learn more about the Low Cost Investment Plan at NAIC's Web Site.

Data

As mentioned briefly in Part II, you have different options for the data you use to complete NAIC's Stock Selection Guide (SSG) and other stock analysis forms. Many people fill out the form using Value Line or S&P data, but there is another, easier way. Individual NAIC members and investment club members have full access to a continuously updated data source through NAIC's Online Premium Services (OPS) for a modest annual fee.

OPS data reports for over 10,000 companies can be downloaded directly into NAIC stock analysis software, offering an almost instantaneous first look at a company's financial fundamentals. You can learn much more about the benefits and uses of OPS in the *NAIC Computerized Investing & the Internet Handbook*.

NAIC's online store

Also available at NAIC's Web Site is NAIC's Online Store, where you can purchase NAIC memberships, books, software, OPS data subscriptions, and even register for NAIC national events such as CompuFest and The *Better Investing* National Convention. You'll find plenty of other educational resources as well; simply browse through the store next time you're online to see what's available.

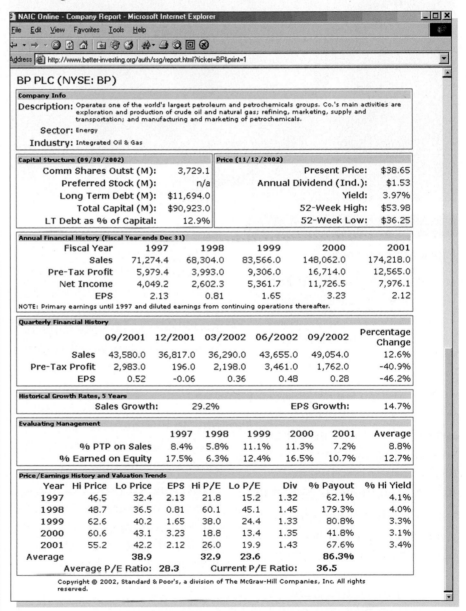

Figure 19-04: A sample OPS company report

NAIC Software

Stock analysis tools

As we covered briefly in Part II, NAIC's Stock Selection Guide (SSG) and other stock analysis tools are available in software form. When you use your computer to complete a Stock Selection Guide (especially if you download the OPS data instead of keying it in by hand), you can generate an overview of the company's financial information in literally seconds.

While you'll still need to do a thorough analysis before deciding that a particular stock is worthy of adding to your portfolio, this quick glance of the chart on page one of the SSG can often be enough to show that you shouldn't bother pursuing a stock any further. If earnings and sales are weak or decreasing year after year, stop your analysis right there and move on to a company with better prospects. SSG software practically automates this initial screening, saving you time you might have otherwise spent entering data or creating graphs only to find the company you're analyzing doesn't meet your requirements.

NAIC offers a variety of stock selection software for you to use on your computer. The section below will give you a very brief overview of your choices. You can learn much more about these different options and how to decide which is best for you in *NAIC Computerized Investing & the Internet Handbook*.

Best for beginners

NAIC Classic was designed specifically for beginning investors. You'll find step-by-step instructions and on-screen help to guide you through your first attempts at using NAIC's stock analysis tools such as the Stock Selection Guide (SSG). *Classic* also teaches the Stock Check List and Stock Comparison Guide forms, and *Classic Plus* adds in the Portfolio Management Guide (PMG) and Portfolio Evaluation and Review Technique (PERT). *Classic* and *Classic Plus* use the on-screen Stock Wiz icon to give you feedback about the critical decisions you need to make within these forms.

Beginning investors can use the tutorial to teach them the basics of NAIC stock analysis. More advanced investors can turn straight to the forms once they've mastered the basics, and can choose to turn the Stock Wiz feature off if they prefer not to use it. The printed user's manual contains written instructions and investment guidance as well.

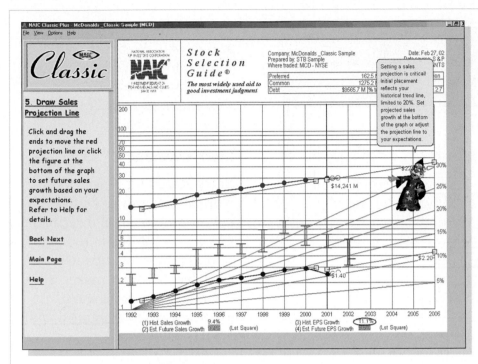

Figure 19-05: Sample page from NAIC Classic *software*

For investors at any level

NAIC offers two versions of stock analysis software to its members, *Investor's Toolkit* and *Stock Analyst*. Both programs allow users to apply NAIC investing principles and include a variety of additional options so investors of any level can customize the software to their needs.

Investor's Toolkit software offers a computerized version of NAIC's stock analysis forms—the Stock Check List, Stock Selection Guide and Stock Comparison Guide. *Toolkit PRO*

also includes NAIC's portfolio management forms: PERT, PERT Worksheets A and B, Portfolio Management Guide, Trend Report, and the Challenger.

If you're a beginning investor or just don't want the portfolio tools yet, you can purchase *Investor's Toolkit* first and add in the PRO component when you're ready. All of the *Toolkit* forms offer context sensitive help and are appropriate for all levels of investors, from novice to advanced. *Toolkit* also comes

with a comprehensive written manual containing detailed information about analyzing stocks using NAIC philosophy.

From the creators of *NAIC Classic* comes *Stock Analyst PLUS!*, with the same stock analysis tools and resources as *Classic Plus*, but with additional graphs and aimed more towards intermediate and advanced investors. In addition to the wide range of NAIC stock selection and portfolio management forms, *Stock Analyst PLUS!* also offers balance sheet and cash flow analysis for investors interested in using this financial information, as well as a retirement planner and a wide range of reports for financial planning.

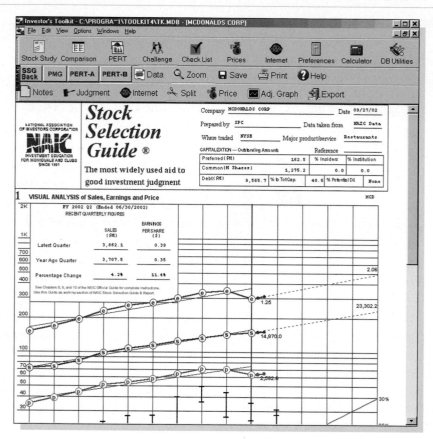

Figure 19-06: Sample page from Investor's Toolkit *software*

information about demo copies at the NAIC Web Site, and more info about all these programs in the *NAIC Computerized Investing & the Internet Handbook.*

Stock screening

Stock screening provides you with an easy way to winnow down your potential investment choices out of the thousands of publicly traded companies available. Software makes this screening process a snap, especially when combined with NAIC's OPS data.

NAIC Stock Prospector allows you to identify companies with financial characteristics you consider important. Prospector displays these companies with

All of NAIC's stock analysis software programs provide valuable assistance to both beginning and experienced investors hoping to make the stock analysis and portfolio management process more efficient by using their computer. The particular program you choose depends on your needs and skill level. If you're not sure which is right for you, consider downloading evaluation versions of the software and trying them all out before you buy. You can find more

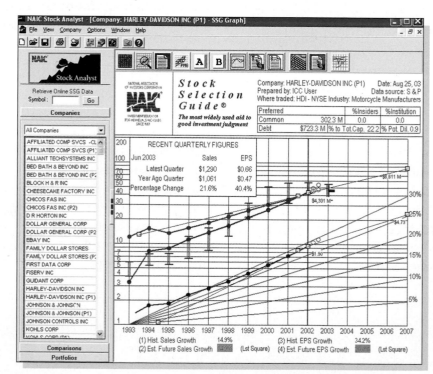

Figure 19-07: Sample page from Stock Analyst Plus *software*

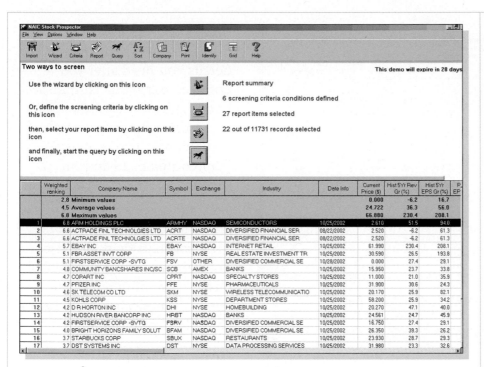

Figure 19-08: Sample view from NAIC Stock Prospector *software*

a mini Stock Selection Guide or graphs of 20 different financial items to help you visualize historical information. You can select, arrange, and display these graphs as easily as flipping pages in a book.

You can screen using 120 different variables, divided into groups such as growth, quality, and value, to help you define your reports and search criteria. *Prospector* will also allow you to define entirely new criteria using your own formulas if you desire. As with *NAIC Classic, Stock Prospector* includes a Wizard with pre-defined reports to help the beginner get started.

Portfolio management tools

It's not enough to learn to analyze and then to purchase stocks for your own personal portfolio. You also need to track your purchases and sales and manage your portfolio with as much care as you select your investments. Portfolio management software can help you take care of all these tasks with ease.

Portfolio Record Keeper (PRK)

NAIC's Portfolio Record Keeper (PRK) offers investors all the tools they need to follow their investments and prepare specialized reports for financial planning and tax preparation needs. You can create multiple portfolios and organize your investments in whichever way is best for you and update the value of all your portfolio holdings automatically online.

PRK is designed to simplify portfolio management and investment record keeping, meaning that you'll spend less time on recordkeeping due to the comprehensive reports you'll have at your fingertips. Better recordkeeping also means less frustration at tax

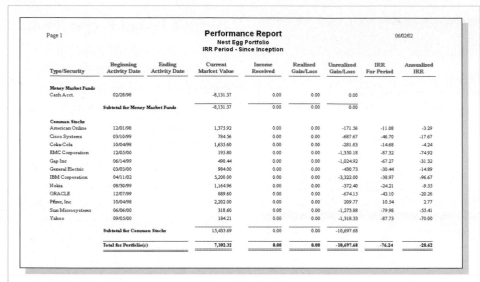

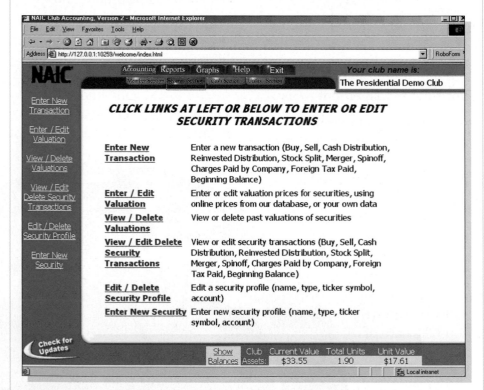

Figure 19-09: Sample report from NAIC's Portfolio Record Keeper

Figure 19-10: Sample page view of NAIC Club Accounting *software*

time, since you'll be able to quickly print out the investment details you need after you've entered your financial transactions. There's no good reason to continue figuring everything by hand when you can use your computer to do your accounting work for you.

PRK allows you to calculate the annualized return of each of your portfolios with one click. You can also create a variety of charts, including ones that show diversification by industry as well as company size.

Investment club accounting tools

Investment club members must be diligent about tracking their investment club portfolio. Some clubs do all the accounting by hand or with homemade spreadsheets, but NAIC offers investment club software and online resources that will take the drudgery and uncertainty out of the investment club accounting process for your club treasurer. Both *NAIC Club Accounting* software *(NCA)* and *NAIC Online Club Accounting (NOCA)* are continuously updated to conform to current IRS regulations, allowing clubs to focus on the work of investing instead of having to keep up with the latest accounting details.

Clubs have the option of choosing either software or online club accounting tools. *NAIC Club Accounting (NCA)* is software that club treasurers install on their own personal computers. Treasurers then can print or e-mail monthly reports for each member, including valuation statements and member status reports.

With *NAIC Online Club Accounting (NOCA)*, club members can access these reports themselves online at any time. The club treasurer inputs transactions online at the *NOCA* Web site, and the records are updated instantly. Each member has the ability to view the club's accounting records in real time, but only the treasurer and other designated officers have the ability to make changes to this information.

Whether clubs choose to keep their records on one computer with *NCA* or to go online with *NOCA*, they can purchase a tax printer subscription each year that works with either option. Computerized records help simplify the club treasurer's job tremendously, and makes the annual financial audit as well as tax preparation much easier than other recordkeeping options.

Figure 19-11: Sample page view of NAIC Online Club Accounting (NOCA)

SITES FOR SUPPORT

Regardless of which NAIC software and online products you use, you'll find much more information about these products at the developers' individual Web sites. You can get technical assistance and support at these sites as well. (A current support contract may be required for some forms of assistance.) You'll find these sites listed in the Online Resource Guide at the end of this book.

Being a Responsible Investor

Introduction

It's not enough to just be an investor. You must also take your role as an investor seriously and be deliberate about keeping on top of paperwork, continuing research and tracking your portfolio to ensure that it's meeting your goals.

You shouldn't set up a 401(k) or automatic mutual fund investment only to ignore it until it's tax time

or you need the money. Portfolio management is just as important as portfolio building. You must do at least a minimum of regular portfolio management, but there's no reason this should be an overwhelming task. This chapter will give you a chance to start thinking about this process.

Schedule your tasks

Becoming a responsible investor doesn't take much work. You can make the process much easier by breaking down your most important investment related tasks into a schedule. The tasks that follow are meant as general guidelines. Some of them may not apply to your situation, or you may have other items to take care of that we don't list here.

The basic concept remains the same regardless of the specific tasks. Identify what you need to do and how often it needs to be done, then schedule appropriately, in tandem with the other items on your monthly, quarterly and annual "to do" lists. Here are some ideas of where to start. Remember that you can find much more detail on the topic of portfolio management in another book in NAIC's educational series, the *NAIC Using Portfolio Management Wisdom Handbook*.

Monthly

1. Enter all investment transactions into your investment recordkeeping software (such as NAIC *Portfolio Record Keeper*) or accounting notebook.

2. Read through any financial statements sent to you by mail or online.

3. Reconcile all brokerage, mutual fund and relevant bank statements against your accounting records.

Quarterly

1. Read any quarterly updates you receive from your investments, looking, for instance, to see whether earnings have increased or decreased.

2. Update Stock Selection Guides for any individual stocks you own with the company's latest financial data (such as earnings). With OPS data, this update can be done almost instantaneously (although it may not always contain recently released data).

Annually

1. Complete your own annual report for your portfolio, including annual returns for all investments and for your portfolio as a whole.

2. Compare your portfolio returns to your financial goals for the year, determining if any changes (in investments or goals) need to be made.

3. Set financial and investment goals for the year ahead, including a plan for how you anticipate meeting those goals. Is there a certain amount of money you'd like to invest over the coming year? Are you working towards a specific financial goal?

4. Read annual reports for your portfolio holdings, both individual stocks and mutual funds, either online or in paper form. If you're especially motivated, read the footnotes as well and learn to interpret their at-times-confusing contents. If you have questions about what you read, simply log onto the I-Club-List or the NAIC Forum on CompuServe and ask for help.

5. Attend annual stockholder meetings for all individual stocks you own whenever possible, or vote the proxy that is mailed to you before each annual meeting.

6. Prepare for tax season by either creating the appropriate reports in *Portfolio Record Keeper* or by gathering the appropriate broker/mutual fund statements and compiling a list of your financial transactions for the year.

7. Archive the previous year's financial statements after tax preparation. Remove them from your current files but keep them someplace accessible in case you need to check something. Some investors keep a back-up copy of their year-end financial reports, either on paper or in electronic form, and store it at an off-site location (such as a safe deposit box) in the event that their original records are lost or destroyed.

Which records to keep, and for how long

How long you should keep old utility bills and credit card receipts is a question you can answer with any decent personal finance book (see Chapter 1 for our suggestions). The answer can be complicated depending on your financial situation and personal preferences, so we won't dive into it at this point. But we can give a brief overview of how you might want to handle your *investment*-related paperwork.

Remember to be conscious of your privacy when discarding any financial paperwork. Never just throw away account statements and bank records or anything else with an account, credit card or your Social Security Number on it. Buy a paper shredder (you can find decent, inexpensive ones at any office supply store) and use it to destroy any document containing financially sensitive information before you recycle or throw it away.

While the chances may be low, it's possible that anyone coming across intact financial records after you've put them in the trash may use that information for unscrupulous purposes. Better to spend an extra few minutes to shred anything even slightly financial in nature than to deal with the potential for identity theft or other similar crimes.

Transaction and dividend reports

Keep all buy and sell transactions for stocks, mutual funds and other investments indefinitely. This is one of those "better safe than sorry" situations. Even if you hold these investments in a tax-deferred account and won't have to worry about calculating the cost basis or capital gains, you should still hang on to these transaction records and dividend statements, just in case.

You also want to be sure to keep anything that shows fees that you paid when buying or selling (such as brokerage fees or mutual fund loads). You may need these amounts to calculate the cost basis (the purchase price minus any expenses or dividends on which taxes have already been paid) of your investments for tax purposes.

This doesn't mean that you have to clutter up the files you use day to day with these or any old records, though. Put them out of the way in a safe place, and then put them out of your mind. Some people

package up all the documents they might need to back up their tax returns, along with annual statements and other financial end-of-year records, and file them away in a manila envelope or banker's box with the year clearly written on the outside. This collection can then be stashed out of sight in a closet or attic somewhere, while still remaining within easy grasp if the need for access arises.

Monthly statements

As soon as you receive a quarterly or annual statement containing the same information, you can safely discard your monthly statements (shredding them first to maintain privacy, of course).

Annual statements

Annual statements from brokerages, mutual fund companies and other investment entities should be kept indefinitely (archived as we describe above so you don't clutter your files). Double-check your monthly or quarterly ending balances against those in the annual statement to ensure that everything reconciles. You may need these annual statements for tax preparation, so keep them close at hand once you receive them in January until after your taxes have been filed and any payment made or refund received.

Quarterly and annual reports

Unless they contain crucial information that you know you'll want to review in the future, you can discard past quarterly and annual reports from your stock and mutual fund holdings after you've read them and voted on any pending shareholder issues. Many investors keep the most current annual and quarterly reports for reference, replacing them as newer reports are released.

If you find you need an old report in the future, chances are excellent that you can access any of the company or fund's recent filings at their Web site. There's little reason to hang on to all those glossy reports and pages of financial reports in tiny type on tissue-thin paper when you shouldn't have much trouble getting the information in other forms if you really need it at some future date.

Tracking your portfolio

Portfolio management is another hallmark trait of the responsible investor. You should regularly review your portfolio to ensure that you're following your own chosen investment philosophy and that you're on track to reach your financial goals. Of course your investments may not always perform as well as you'd hope in the short term, but it's important to try to determine if that's because of a depressed overall market condition or because you've chosen substandard investments.

Good portfolio management means tracking your stocks and mutual funds on an annual (at minimum) or quarterly (best option when possible) basis. Check to make sure that a stock's earnings and sales are in line with your projections. You'll also want to know if a mutual fund's investment choices have veered away from its stated strategy, or if there's been a change in fund management.

NAIC's analysis and portfolio management tools can help you follow your stock and mutual fund investments in a careful and regular fashion. You can find detailed instructions for using these tools, either with software or by hand with the paper forms, in the *NAIC Using Portfolio Management Wisdom Handbook*. Software such as *NAIC's Portfolio Record Keeper (PRK)* can also help you keep watch over your portfolio as a whole as well as your individual investments.

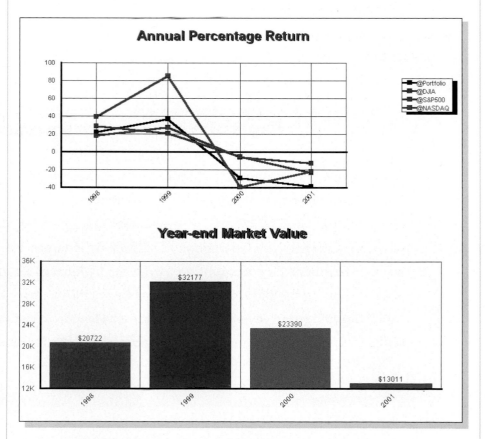

Figure 20-01: Sample report from NAIC's *Portfolio Record Keeper*

Key traits of a responsible investor

- Ask questions until the answers make sense to you

- Thoroughly research stocks and mutual funds (including reading the annual report and fund prospectus) before investing

- Maintain and regularly update accurate records

- Understand your investments so that you know what you're investing in

- Vote your proxies (stock and mutual fund)

- Attend shareholder meetings whenever possible (even if only just once)

- File taxes accurately and on time

- Invest regularly according to your investment philosophy and financial goals

- Analyze your portfolio regularly, using NAIC portfolio management tools if desired

- Sell when necessary, according to your investment philosophy

A final word (or two)

Congratulations on making your financial education a priority by reading this book! Now it's time to move on to more advanced investing topics. Depending on your needs and interests, choose another book from this educational series and expand your horizons even more. Good luck with what we hope will be both a personal and financial journey.

NAIC'S BETTER INVESTING BOOK SERIES

NAIC Offical Guide Introduction to Successful Investing *Handbook* by Angele McQuade

NAIC Stock Selection *Handbook* by Bonnie Biafore

NAIC Mutual Fund *Handbook* by Amy Crane

NAIC Investment Club Operations *Handbook* by Jonathan Katz

NAIC Investment Club Accounting *Handbook* by Richard Beaubien and Matt Stoller

NAIC Investing for Life - *Youth Handbook* by Fritz Williams

NAIC Computerized Investing & the Internet *Handbook* by Douglas Gerlach

NAIC Using Portfolio Management Wisdom *Handbook* by Bonnie Biafore, Beth Hamm, Peggy Schmeltz, and Betty Taylor

Meet an NAIC Investment Club Member

Ann Dexheimer
Pleasanton, CA

Ann Dexheimer started investing 10 years ago after making a horrible discovery. Her financial advisor was under investigation by the SEC for stealing more than $75,000 Ann had thought was invested in government bonds. Her advisor covered up the thefts with fake statements, so Ann had no clue about the deception until attorneys from the SEC contacted her.

This expensive wake-up call led Ann to realize that by giving her financial advisor complete control over her investments, she'd willingly given up all responsibility for her own money. Determined not to put herself in a situation where she could be taken advantage of financially again, Ann began reading financial magazines as a start to her financial education. An article on investment clubs in *Money* magazine inspired her to organize her friends, and they all joined NAIC. Ann bought her very first share of stock through NAIC's Low Cost Investment Plan, her hands shaking as she wrote out the check. Ann has made incredible progress since that first experience of investing on her own, and now generously shares what she's learned with other investors. She recommends that beginning investors take some time to get used to all the new financial terms and concepts they encounter. Time isn't the only important factor, though. New investors must also be willing to put in some "mental elbow grease", as Ann puts it, to make real progress. This effort will pay off, both educationally and financially.

Ann says that the hardest investing lesson she's learned is that choosing to use a financial advisor doesn't free you from taking ultimate responsibility for your own financial situation. No one will watch your money as well as you will, she cautions.

Ann recovered only $5,000 of the $75,000 her financial advisor stole from her. As difficult as the loss was, Ann still considers it the best life lesson she's ever received. Ann now shares that lesson and many others with new investors as a volunteer with NAIC's San Francisco regional chapter. If she'd known how interesting the world of investing was, Ann says, she'd have started her financial education much earlier. She's turned the lesson of a lifetime into an unexpected and entirely fulfilling new way of life.

Appendix

Appendix A:

Online Resource Guide

Visit these Web sites for more information on many of the subjects covered in this book.

NAIC-related sites

NAIC home page

NAIC's official site, containing educational resources for investors and investment clubs
www.better-investing.org

NAIC online communities

NAIC Forum on CompuServe
http://go.compuserve.com/NAIC

NAIC e-mail lists
http://lists.better-investing.org

NAIC software developers:

ICLUBcentral

Creator and supporter of several official NAIC software products, including *NAIC Club Accounting (NCA), NAIC Online Club Accounting (NOCA), NAIC Classic products, Stock Analyst Plus, NAIC Investor's Toolkit, NAIC Take Stock* and *NAIC Stock Prospector.*
www.iclub.com

Investment-related sites

Quant IX

Creator of NAIC's *Portfolio Record Keeper*
www.quantix.com

Brokerage research
www.Gomez.com

College savings

www.irs.gov—government regulations for ESAs

www.irs.gov/pub/irs-pdf/p970.pdf—link to download of IRS Publication 970 Tax Benefits for Higher Education

detailed information on both Section 529 plans and ESAs

www.collegesavings.org—information about Section 529 plans from the National Association of State Treasurers

Dividend Reinvestment Plans (DRIPs) and related brokerage options
www.buyandhold.com
www.dripcentral.com
www.sharebuilder.com

Financial planner research

Financial Planning Association
www.fpanet.org

National Association of Personal Financial Advisors
www.napfa.org

Investment regulation

Official site of the Securities and Exchange Commission, where you'll find regulations regarding finding new investment club members
www.sec.gov

Real Estate Investment Trusts (REITS)

National Association of Real Estate Investment Trusts (NAREIT)
www.nareit.com

Taxes

Official site of the Internal Revenue Service, where you'll find useful tax information relating to investment clubs and partnerships
www.irs.gov

THIS AGREEMENT OF PARTNERSHIP, effective as of   (date)   by and between the undersigned, to wit: {names of partners}

NOW, THEREFORE IT IS AGREED:

1. Formation.
The undersigned hereby form a General Partnership in accordance with and subject to the laws of the State of Michigan.

2. Name.
The name of the partnership shall be Mutual Investment Club of Detroit.

3. Term.
The partnership shall begin on   (date)   and shall continue until December 31 of the same year and thereafter from year to year unless earlier terminated as hereinafter provided.

4. Purpose.
The only purpose of the partnership is to invest the assets of the partnership solely in stocks, bonds and other securities ("securities") for the education and benefit of the partners.

5. Meetings.
Periodic meetings shall be held as determined by the partnership.

6. Capital Contributions.
The partners may make capital contributions to the partnership on the date of each periodic meeting in such amounts as the partnership shall determine; provided, however, that no partner's capital account shall exceed twenty percent (20 percent) of the capital accounts of all partners.

7. Value of the Partnership.
The current value of the assets of the partnership, less the current value of the liabilities of the partnership, (hereinafter referred to as the "value of the partnership") shall be determined as of a regularly scheduled date and time ("valuation date") preceding the date of each periodic meeting determined by the Club.

8. Capital Accounts.
A capital account shall be maintained in the name of each partner. Any increase or decrease in the value of the partnership on any valuation date shall be credited or debited, respectively, to each partner's capital account on that date. Any other method of valuing each partner's capital account may be substituted for this method, provided the substituted method results in exactly the same valuation as previously provided herein. Each partner's contribution to, or capital withdrawal from, the partnership shall be credited, or debited, respectively, to that partner's capital account.

9. Management.
Each partner shall participate in the management and conduct of the affairs of the partnership in proportion to his capital account. Except as otherwise determined, all decisions shall be made by the partners whose capital accounts total a majority of the value of the capital accounts of all the partners.

10. Sharing of Profits and Losses.
Net profits and losses of the partnership shall inure to, and be borne by, the partners, in proportion to the value of each of their capital accounts.

11. Books of Account.
Books of account of the transactions of the partnership shall be kept and at all times be available and open to inspection and examination by any partner.

12. Annual Accounting.
Each calendar year, a full and complete account of the condition of the partnership shall be made to the partners.

13. Bank Account.

The partnership may select a bank for the purpose of opening a bank account. Funds in the bank account shall be withdrawn by checks signed by any partner designated by the partnership.

14. Broker Account.

None of the partners of this partnership shall be a broker. However, the partnership may select a broker and enter into such agreements with the broker as required for the purchase or sale of securities. Securities owned by the partnership shall be registered in the partnership name unless another name shall be designated by the partnership.

Any corporation or transfer agent called upon to transfer any securities to or from the name of the partnership shall be entitled to rely on instructions or assignments signed by any partner without inquiry as to the authority of theperson(s) signing such instructions or assignments, or as to the validity of any transfer to or from the name of the partnership.

At the time of a transfer of securities, the corporation or transfer agent is entitled to assume (1) that the partnership is still in existence and (2) that this Agreement is in full force and effect and has not been amended unless the corporation has received written notice to the contrary.

15. No Compensation.

No partner shall be compensated for services rendered to the partnership, except reimbursement for expenses.

16. Additional Partners.

Additional partners may be admitted at any time, upon the unanimous consent of the partners, so long as the number of partners does not exceed twenty five (25).

16A. Transfers to a Trust.

A partner may, after giving written notice to the other partners, transfer his interest in the partnership to a revocable living trust of which he is the grantor and sole trustee.

16B. Removal of a Partner.

Any partner may be removed by agreement of the partners whose capital accounts total a majority of the value of all partners' capital accounts. Written notice of a meeting where removal of a partner is to be considered shall include a specific reference to this matter. The removal shall become effective upon payment of the value of the removed partner's capital account, which shall be in accordance with the provisions on full withdrawal of a partner noted in paragraphs 18 and 20. The vote action shall be treated as receipt of request for withdrawal.

17. Termination of Partnership.

The partnership may be terminated by agreement of the partners whose capital accounts total a majority in value of the capital accounts of all the partners. Written notice of a meeting where termination of the partnership is to be considered shall include a specific reference to this matter. The partnership shall terminate upon a majority vote of all partners' capital accounts. Written notice of the decision to terminate the partnership shall be given to all the partners. Payment shall then be made of all the liabilities of the partnership and a final distribution of the remaining assets either in cash or in kind, shall promptly be made to the partners or their personal representatives in proportion to each partner's capital account.

18. Voluntary Withdrawal (Partial or Full) of a Partner.

Any partner may withdraw a part or all of the value of his capital account in the partnership and the partnership shall continue as a taxable entity. The partner withdrawing a part or all of the value of his capital account shall give notice of such intention in writing to the Secretary. Written notice shall be deemed to be received as of the first meeting of the partnership at which it is presented. If written notice is received between meetings it will be treated as received at the first following meeting.

In making payment, the value of the partnership as set forth in the valuation statement prepared for the first meeting following the meeting at which notice is received from a partner requesting a partial or full withdrawal, will be used to determine the value of the partner's account.

The partnership shall pay the partner who is withdrawing a portion or all of the value of his capital account in the partnership in accordance with paragraph 20 of this Agreement.

19. Death or Incapacity of a Partner.

In the event of the death or incapacity of a partner (or the death or incapacity of the grantor and sole trustee of a revocable living trust, if such trust is partner pursuant to Paragraph 16A hereof), receipt of notice shall be treated as a notice of full withdrawal.

20. Terms of Payment.

In the case of a partial withdrawal, payment may be made in cash or securities of the partnership or a mix of each at the option of the partner making the partial withdrawal. In the case of a full withdrawal, payment may be made in cash or securities or a mix of each at the option of the remaining partners. In either case, where securities are to be distributed, the remaining partners select the securities.

Where cash is transferred, the partnership shall transfer to the partner (or other appropriate entity) withdrawing a portion or all of his interest in the partnership, an amount equal to the lesser of (i) ninety-seven percent (97 percent) of the value of the capital account being withdrawn, or (ii) the value of the capital account being withdrawn, less the actual cost to the partnership of selling securities to obtain cash to meet the withdrawal. The amount being withdrawn shall be paid within 10 days after the valuation date used in determining the withdrawal amount.

If the partner withdrawing a portion or all of the value of his capital account in the partnership desires an immediate payment in cash, the partnership at its earliest convenience may pay eighty percent (80 percent) of the estimated value of his capital account and settle the balance in accordance with the valuation and payment procedures set forth in paragraphs 18 and 20.

Where securities are transferred, the partnership shall select securities to transfer equal to the value of the capital account or a portion of the capital account being withdrawn (i.e., without a reduction for broker commissions). Securities shall be transferred as of the date of the club's valuation statement prepared to determine the value of that partner's capital account in the partnership. The Club's broker shall be advised that ownership of the securities has been transferred to the partner as of the valuation date used for the withdrawal.

21. Forbidden Acts.

No partner shall:

Have the right or authority to bind or obligate the partnership to any extent whatsoever with regard to any matter outside the scope of the partnership purpose.

Except as provided in paragraph 16A, without the unanimous consent of all the other partners, assign, transfer, pledge, mortgage or sell all or part of his interest in the partnership to any other partner or other person whomsoever, or enter into any agreement as the result of which any person or persons not a partner shall become interested with him in the partnership.

Purchase an investment for the partnership where less than the full purchase price is paid for same.

Use the partnership name, credit, or property for other than partnership purposes.

Do any act detrimental to the interests of the partnership or which would make it impossible to carry on the business or affairs of the partnership.

This Agreement of Partnership shall be binding upon the respective heirs, executors, administrators, and personal representatives of the partners.

The partners have caused this Agreement of Partnership to be executed on the dates indicated below, effective as of the date indicated above.

Partners:
{Signatures of partners}

Glossary

Accelerated Depreciation
The amount of expense charged against earnings by a company to write off the cost of a plant or machine over its useful live, giving consideration to wear and tear, obsolescence, and salvage value.

Account Maintenance Fees
A fee an investor pays to a fund company or broker in return for account services.

Accounts Payable
A current liability. Debts owed by a company to its suppliers that must be paid within the course of a year.

Accounts Receivable
A current asset. Debts owed to a company by its customers that the company expects to collect within the course of a year.

Accrued Taxes
A current tax liability owed by an individual or company to various governmental bodies.

Accrued Wages, Interest & Other Expenses
Current liabilities. Money owed by a company to its employees, other businesses (i.e. banks) and miscellaneous expenses.

Accumulated Profits
Same as retained earnings.

Acid Test Ratio
The sum of a company's cash, accounts receivable and marketable securities, divided by its total current liabilities.

Acquisitions
The purchase of one company by another for the purpose of gaining access to different, new or complimentary products or technologies.

Active Portfolio Strategy
Uses strategies and information to achieve better performance than a mutual fund portfolio that passively manages a broadly diversified portfolio, i.e. an index fund.

Actively Managed Mutual Fund
A mutual fund with a manager who uses strategies and information to achieve better performance than a particular market index.

Adviser
The company that manages a fund's portfolio. The adviser makes the portfolio buy and sell decisions in an effort to carry out the fund's investment objective. The investment adviser is also known as the management company. See also investment adviser.

After Tax Return
The return an investor receives on an investment after applicable taxes are paid.

Aggressive Growth Fund
A fund that seeks maximum capital appreciation by purchasing stocks believed to offer potential for rapid growth. These funds also can invest in smaller emerging companies that may not have a proven track record of increasing sales and earnings.

American Depository Receipts (ADRs)
Stock representing specific shares in a foreign corporation.

Amortization.
Reduction of debt through periodic payments consisting of interest and part of the principal.

Analyst
An employee of a mutual fund adviser who analyzes companies for possible fund purchase.

Annual Report
A report issued by a mutual fund detailing a fund's performance, expenses and holdings during a particular year.

Annuity
An insurance product in the form of a contract that provides a series of income payments made at regular intervals during a set period (such as retirement) in return for a premium (or premiums) paid. An annuity usually offers tax-deferral benefits.

Application
A form investors need to fill out when applying to open a mutual fund account.

Asked Price
The price demanded by a willing seller.

Asset
Property or items of value owned by a company, or the economic resources of a business.

Asset Allocation
The practice of dividing personal assets among differing investing vehicles.

Asset Allocation Fund
A fund that spreads its portfolio out among a wide range of different investments. These can include U.S. and overseas stocks, bonds, real estate and gold.

Authorized Stock
The total number of shares that a corporation, as indicated in its charter, is authorized to sell.

Automatic Reinvestment Plan (Dividend Reinvestment)
A fund service that provides shareholders with the option to automatically invest their income dividends and capital gain distributions, also known as a dividend reinvestment plan.

Average Credit Quality
Assesses the overall credit quality of a bond fund's portfolio. To calculate this number, Morningstar averages the credit rating of each bond in the portfolio.

Average Effective Duration
Provides a measurement of a fund's sensitivity to interest-rate changes.

Average Effective Maturity
A measurement of the average maturity of the bonds in a bond fund portfolio.

Average P/E Ratio
As defined by Morningstar, a fund's weighted P/E average, which is calculated by using current stock prices divided by the company's projected earnings.

Averages
Selected lists of stock or bonds whose price action is considered representative of the market as a whole. The best-known averages are the Dow Jones and Standard & Poor's.

Back-end Load Fund
A mutual fund that charges shareholders a fee (commission) to sell shares. This charge decreases the longer the investor holds the shares, eventually zeroing-out.

Balance Sheet
A financial statement detailing, as of a certain point in time, a company's assets, liabilities, and capital.

Balanced Fund
A fund that maintains a portfolio that is divided into a certain percentage of stocks and a certain percentage of bonds.

Basis
The price an investor pays for a security plus any commissions, sales charges or other out-of-pocket expenses.

Bear
An investor who anticipates a market decline.

Bear Market
A market where stock prices have declined 20 percent from a recent high.

Benchmark
The performance of a group of securities used for comparison purposes Through such a comparison, you can determine if your fund outperforms the index over the long-term.

Beta
A coefficient that measures volatility relative to the total market, usually as represented by the S&P 500.

Better Investing Magazine
NAIC's monthly magazine, containing investment information, educational articles and other investment-related resources and news.

Better Investing National Convention
Annual NAIC investment conference featuring educational seminars and corporate exhibits, hosted by NAIC's National Investors Association Advisory Board.

Bid Price
The price offered by a willing buyer.

BITS
NAIC's online newsletter, focused on using computers and the Internet as investing aids.

Blend Style of Investing
This investing style combines elements of the growth and value styles of investing.

Blue Chip
The common stock of a well-known company that has a long record of growth and a reputation for quality management.

Board of Directors
The body that oversees a fund's activities and contracts with the management company, distributor, custodian and transfer agent to run the fund.

Bond
A debt instrument. When a company issues bonds, it agrees to pay bondholders a stated rate of interest until the principal is repaid on a specified date.

Bond Fund
A fund with a portfolio consisting primarily of corporate, municipal or U.S. Government bonds. These funds focus on income potential rather than growth.

Bond Index Fund
A bond fund based on a bond index. Managers of such funds invest their assets according to the particular index followed by the fund.

Bond Ratings
An assessment of the solvency of a particular company in terms of its ability to pay interest and repay principle to bond holders.

Bond Ratio
That portion of a company's capital structure consisting of bonds, found by dividing the face value of bonds by the total value of bonds, preferred stock, common stock, capital surplus and retained earnings.

Bondholder
A creditor.

Book Value (Common Stock)
The value of common stock of a company, found by adding the par value of the common stock, retained earnings, and surplus reserves.

Broker
A firm or individual that arranges a transfer of securities between a buyer and a seller, charging a fee for the service.

Brokerage Commission
A sales fee charged in return for investment advice and/or the buying and selling of fund shares.

Brokerage House
A firm whose employees (brokers) arrange the transfer of securities between a buyer and a seller, charging a fee for the service.

Bull Market
A period of generally rising market prices.

Business Cycle
The phases of transition in a free economy, consisting of prosperity, recession, depression, and recovery.

Buy and Hold Philosophy
A philosophy that can be adopted by individual investors or fund managers that involves purchasing stocks and retaining them for the long term.

Buy Zone
The computed range on NAIC forms that signals favorable buy prices for the analyzed security.

Bylaws (See Club Operating Procedures.)

Capital Appreciation
An investment gain from the price appreciation of a security.

Capital Gain or Capital Loss
Profit or loss from the sale of a capital asset, such as a security.

Capital Gains Distribution
Shareholders receive these distributions when a fund manager sells stock held in the portfolio at a profit.

Capital Structure
The total of bonds, preferred stock, common stock and retained earnings.

Capitalism
An economic system that permits private, rather than government ownership of the means of production, and free pricing of products.

Capitalist
Anyone who provides funds for the conduct of a business.

Capitalization
The total value, as stated in a company's books, of bonds, preferred and common stock and retained earnings.

Cash
This includes actual cash held by a fund and cash equivalents. Cash equivalents include money market or other fixed income securities with maturities of less than one year.

Cash Dividend
A portion of the net earnings or retained earnings of a corporation directed by the board to be paid to the stockholders in cash.

Cash Flow
The net income of a company, with the addition of any non-cash deductions from income such as depreciation and depletion.

Cash Flow Statement
A report showing a company's cash flow over selected periods of time.

Cash Reserves
Cash or short-term securities held by a mutual fund.

Cheap Stock
Not necessarily a low-priced stock, but one that is selling at a lower price/earnings ratio than would appear justified by corporate results.

Chief Executive Officer (CEO)
The head of a company's business operations.

Class A Shares
Investors who purchase these shares are assessed a sales charge (commission) which is taken right off the top of their initial investment. Also known as a front-end load.

Class B Shares
A mutual fund that charges investors a fee (commission) to sell shares. Class B shares have a bank-end load charge that is also known as a contingent deferred sales charge.

Class C Shares
These funds charge a sales fee (commission) annually and are also known as Class C shares. Such shares cannot be converted to another share class.

Closed-end Investment Company (or Fund)
A company or fund that has a relatively fixed number of shares that are bought or sold on the stock exchanges. A closed-end fund's price is determined by supply and demand.

Club Operating Procedures
A set of rules and regulations created by investment club members to define their club's day-to-day business operations as well as individual member responsibilities.

Club Treasurers List
An e-mail list where NAIC investment club treasurers can ask for advice regarding club accounting issues.

Commission
A sales fee charged in return for investment advice and/or the buying and selling of stock.

Commission Free Brokerage Trades
A brokerage trade that is executed without a commission or fee.

Common Stock
A representation of ownership in a corporation.

Common Stock Ratio
That portion of a company's capital structure consisting of common stock.

Compounded Annual Return
The yearly rate of return that is earned or paid and that usually is compounded daily, monthly, or yearly.

Compounding
Earnings that are generated from the return on an investment.

CompuFest
Annual NAIC investment education conference focusing on computers and investing, hosted by NAIC's Computer Group Advisory Board.

Consolidated Statement
A statement that includes figures for a company and all of its subsidiaries.

Contingent Deferred Sales Charge
A commission or back-end load that may be imposed on fund shares sold within a certain period of time. Also known as a back-end load or Class B shares.

Convertible Preferred Stock
A type of security that can be exchanged for a set amount of common stock at a preset price.

Corporate Bonds
Bonds issued by U.S. and foreign corporations.

Corporate High Yield Bonds
Bonds issued by corporations with below investment grade credit ratings.

Corporation
An entity created by law with perpetual life and limited liability of shareholders.

Cost Basis
The price an investor pays for a security plus any commissions, sales charges or other out-of-pocket expenses.

Cost of Goods Sold
The cost of labor, materials and overhead that properly may be assigned to units produced.

Cost of Sales
Same as cost of goods sold.

Country-Specific Fund
A mutual fund that invests its assets in the stocks of one particular foreign country.

Coverdell Education Savings Account (ESA)
Formerly known as Education IRAs, these are individually established college savings plans.

Creditor
An individual or entity that lends money to a company, e.g., a bondholder, buyer of commercial paper, or extender of trade credit.

Current Asset
An asset that can be converted into cash within a year.

Current Liability
A liability of a company that must be paid within one year.

Current Ratio
A firm's current assets divided by its current liabilities.

Current Yield
The annual income yielded by a security, divided by its current price. For stock investors, the current yield is also known as the dividend yield.

Custodial Fees
The fees charged by a mutual fund to compensate the company that maintains a mutual fund's assets, including its portfolio of securities or the records of the portfolio.

Cyclical
A trend or process that moves in a cycle. The stock market follows a cyclical pattern from a bull market to a bear market and back to a bull market.

Cyclical Growth Stock
A stock that is very dependent on the business cycle, and reaches new highs in sales and earnings in each succeeding period of prosperity.

Cyclical Industry
An industry that follows a boom-bust pattern in a regular market cycle.

Debenture
A bond not secured by any specific property but backed only by the general credit of the issuing company.

Deferred Charge
Also known as deferred expense or prepaid expense, an asset that represents payment for a good or service properly chargeable to a future period.

Deferred Expense
Same as deferred charge.

Defined Benefit Pension
A retirement plan that promises to pay a certain amount, usually based on the number of years employed and salary level.

Defined Contribution Pension
A retirement plan with a fixed contribution rate, where benefits employees receive after retirement depend to some extent upon the contributions and their earnings.

Depletion
A charge against earnings derived from a natural resource. Lumber and oil companies are among those listing depletion on their balance sheets.

Depreciation
The amount of expense charged against earnings by a company to write off the cost of a plant or machine over its useful live, giving consideration to wear and tear, obsolescence, and salvage value.

Derivatives
A financial security whose value is determined in part by the value and characteristics of another underlying security.

Dilution
The effect on earnings and book value per share when the number of shares issued by a company increases disproportionately to growth in company earnings or assets.

Direct Stock Purchase Plans (DSPs)
An investment plan similar to a Dividend Reinvestment Plan but by which investors are able to purchase initial shares of a company directly through the company or its agent rather than through an outside broker.

Discount Broker
A broker who provides services at a price discounted from that of a full-service broker.

Discount Brokerage
A brokerage firm that provides services at a price discounted from that of a full-service brokerage.

Distributor
A company that initially underwrites a mutual fund's shares. Distributors also buy shares directly from the fund and resell them to investors.

Diversification
The practice of spreading investments among a range of different securities to reduce risk.

Diversified Portfolio
A portfolio that invests in many companies in an effort to reduce risk.

Dividend
A payment a company makes, in cash or stock, to its shareholders.

Dividend Per Share
The total dividend paid divided by the number of shares of common stock outstanding.

Dividend Reinvestment Plan (DRIPs)
A fund service that provides shareholders with the option to automatically invest their income dividends and capital gain distributions.

Dividend Yield
Found by dividing the cash dividend per share by market price per share. Lower yields are associated with growth companies and higher yields with more mature companies.

Dollar Cost Averaging
Buying a set dollar amount of a security at stated intervals.

Dow Jones Industrial Average
An index of 30 blue chip U.S. stocks, maintained by the editors of the *Wall Street Journal*.

Downside Risk
On NAIC forms, the difference between present price and estimated low price for the next five years.

Earned Surplus
Profits that have been kept in the business rather than being distributed as dividends, also called undistributed earnings or profits, accumulated profits, retained earnings, or retained income.

Earnings
A company's profit after taxes.

Earnings Per Share (EPS)
A company's net income divided by the number of shares of common stock outstanding.

Earnings Plowback
Reinvesting earnings in a business rather than paying them out to stockholders in the form of dividends.

Earnings Report
A financial statement (also called income statement or profit and loss statement) that shows a company's operating results over a period of time and gives evidence of the company's profitability.

Economies of Scale
Savings realized by larger corporations, which are able to spread fixed costs over a larger number of units produced.

Electronic Communications Network
A computer network that processes stock buy and sell orders by matching them electronically.

Electronic Signature
A way to legally sign documents sent electronically.

Equity
An ownership interest held by shareholders in a corporation. (See Stock.)

Equity Capital
Funds raised by the owners of a business.

Exchange
A meeting place for the representatives of buyers and sellers of securities.

Exchange Fee
A fee some mutual fund families charge for investors to exchange their shares in one mutual fund for another fund in the same family.

Exchange Traded Funds
An index-based mutual fund that trades like a stock on a stock exchange throughout the day. Unlike traditional mutual funds that are valued at the end of each trading day, the share price of Exchange Traded Funds fluctuates.

Ex-dividend
When a stock is selling ex-dividend, the buyer does not receive the soon-to-be paid dividend. The dividend remains the property of the seller.

Expenses
Any of the sum of fees imposed by a mutual fund on its shareholders.

Expense Ratio
The ratio of investor expenses to net assets of the fund. The expense ratio does not include brokerage costs or loads.

FIFO
Abbreviation for first in, first out, a method of inventory valuation.

Family of Funds
A group of mutual funds managed by the same company.

Fee-Only Financial Planner
A professional financial planner who charges a flat fee rather than a commission based on investments sold.

Financial Leverage
Same as leverage.

Financial Planner
A professional who provides investing information and advice. Financial Planners and Certified Financial Planners (CFA) will either charge a flat fee for their advice or will get a sales commission in return for placing investors' money in particular mutual funds.

Financial Risk
One of the important types of risk confronting investors, it acknowledges that companies may suffer adversity that would affect their ability to make payments to investors and/or creditors.

Financial Statement
A report depicting a corporation's or fund company's financial condition as of a given date or financial results for a given period. The most common financial statements are the balance sheet, income statement, and cash flow statement.

Fiscal Period
A span of time selected as an accounting period.

Fixed Asset
Tangible property owned by a company that is utilized in the production of net income, but is not expected to be consumed or converted into cash.

Fixed Asset Turnover
A measurement of efficiency, found by dividing fixed assets before depreciation into net sales.

Fixed Cost
A business expense that continues even if production ceases.

Fixed Income Investments
Those investments, including bonds and (usually) preferred stock, for which the company is committed to paying a specific amount of return to investors.

Fixed Liability
A debt of a company that will not be paid for a year or more.

401(k) Plan
An employer-sponsored retirement plan. Such plans allow employees to make tax-deferred contributions into the plan, which in some cases are matched by the employer.

403(b) Plan
An employer-sponsored retirement plan available to employees of educational institutions and non-profit organizations.

Foreign Bonds
Bonds issued by companies based outside the United States.

Foreign Currencies
The money issued by foreign countries.

Foreign Stocks
Companies that are based outside the United States.

Forms 10-K and 10-Q
A mutual fund's annual and quarterly reports, filing requirements of the Securities and Exchange Commission.

Form 1065
A tax form that must be filed by all investment clubs operating as partnerships.

Formula Investing
Investing by prearranged design. Dollar cost averaging is a popular type of formula investing.

Fractional Shares
A partial share of a mutual fund or stock.

Free Enterprise
Same as Capitalism.

Front-End Load
A sales charge that is assessed when a fund investment is made.

Front-End Load Mutual Fund
A mutual fund that assesses a sales charge when a fund investment is made.

Full Service Broker
A broker that charges a higher commission than a discount broker in return for a higher level of service.

Fund Asset Size
The amount of assets in a mutual fund.

Funded Debt
Long-term debt (maturing after more than one year), usually issued as a bond.

Fund Exchanges
Many fund families allow investors to exchange their shares in one fund within a family for another fund within the same family.

Funding
The refinancing of debt, prior to maturity (same as refunding).

Fund Share Classes
Many fund companies sell different classes of the same fund shares. For individual investors, these classes are Class A, which carry a front-end load, Class B, which carry a back-end load, and Class C, which carry a level load.

Fund Shares Outstanding
The number of shares issued by the fund company to fund shareholders.

Fund Manager's Letter
This is part of the Shareholder Report where the fund manager comments on the fund's recent performance and strategy as well as the general economic outlook.

Fund Statements
Fund companies issue statements regularly to all shareholders. These inform shareholders about their fund holdings, performance, net asset value and the overall value of their funds.

Fund Supermarkets
These are mutual fund companies or brokerages that offer a large variety of mutual funds to investors.

Fund Transfers
Sending money electronically from one account to another.

Futures
Contracts to buy and sell commodities (items that will be mined or grown).

General Accounting Office
The investigative arm of the U.S. Congress.

Global Bond Funds
Bond funds that invest their assets in any country around the world.

Global Fund
A mutual fund that invests in both U.S. and foreign securities.

Government Bond
U.S. government debt, offering what experts consider the lowest possible financial risk.

Government Bond Fund General
A bond fund with a portfolio invested in treasuries, mortgage-backed securities and governmental agency securities.

Government Bond Fund Treasury
A bond fund with a portfolio solely made up of Treasury bond, bills and notes.

Governmental Agency Securities
A bond, bill or note issued by an agency of the Federal Government.

Gross Domestic Product
The new statistic offered by the U.S. government to supplant Gross National Product.

Gross Profit
Net sales minus cost of goods sold.

Gross Profit Margin
Gross profit divided by net sales, also called gross margin.

Gross Sales
Sales before deductions for returns and allowances.

Growth Fund
A fund with an objective of long-term growth of capital. Managers of such funds invest in common stocks with significant growth potential.

Growth and Income Fund
A fund that has a portfolio that holds companies with both growth potential and dividend income.

Growth Manager
A fund manager who invests in companies that demonstrate higher than average sales and earnings growth.

Growth Stock
Companies that show higher than average growth in sales and earnings. Growth is fueled by a number of different elements, including superior management, new products, expanding markets or the discovery of new resources.

Growth Style of Investing
Managers who follow this style of investing seek companies with consistent, above average sales and earnings growth in an effort to produce long-term growth of capital.

Goodwill
An intangible asset that arises from business combinations accounted for under the purchase method and represents the cost to a purchaser in excess of the fair value of net tangible assets (equity) of an acquired business.

Government Securities
U.S. Government obligations (bills, notes, and bonds).

Hedge Fund
A mutual fund which hedges its market commitments by holding securities it believes are likely to increase in value while short-selling securities it believes are likely to decrease in value.

Hidden Asset
An asset such as a trade secret, or other intangible, that does not appear on a company's books.

High-Yield Bond Fund
A bond fund with a portfolio of non-investment grade bonds that pays a high interest rate compared to other bond funds. High-yield bond funds are also known as junk bond funds.

Hold Zone
On NAIC forms, the calculated price range where securities are neither a buy nor a sell.

Holdings
All of the securities held by an individual, mutual fund or institution.

Hot Tip
A story suggesting a favorable development for a company.

Hybrid Funds
A fund that maintains a portfolio strictly divided between stocks and bonds. These funds are also known as balanced funds.

I-Club-List
An e-mail list where NAIC-style investors discuss a variety of investment topics.

Income
An amount of money received in return for making an investment or doing a job.

Income Fund
A fund that seeks income by investing in stocks and bonds that pay high dividends and interest.

Income Return
The portion of a fund's total return that derives from interest distributions.

Income Statement
A financial statement, also called a *profit and loss statement*, which reports income, costs, expenses and profits (losses) over a period, usually one full year.

Income Stock
A stock offering an above-average cash dividend yield.

Index Fund
A fund with the goal of replicating the performance of a particular market index. Index funds are not actively managed. Their performance usually lags their respective index by the fund's expense ratio.

Individual Retirement Account (IRA)
A personal, tax-deferred retirement account. Taxes on capital are deferred until you withdraw money, usually at retirement.

Inflation
An increase in the cost of consumer goods, which leads to a decline in the purchasing power of the dollar.

Initial Public Offering (IPO)
The first time a stock or closed-end mutual fund is offered to the investing public.

Institutional Funds
Mutual funds designed for wealthy investors or managers of large organizations who have large sums of money to invest. Minimum investment requirements for institutional funds can be in the tens of thousands or hundreds of thousands of dollars.

Institutional Investors
Wealthy investors or managers of large institutions such as pension funds that have large sums of money to invest in the markets.

Insolvency
The condition that exists when a corporation's liabilities exceed assets, and it is not able to pay its debts.

International Bond Funds
Bond funds that invest their assets outside of the United States.

Interest
A payment made to a creditor by a borrower for the use of money.

Interest Rate
A percentage rate at which money can be lent or borrowed. In the United States, the Federal Reserve sets interest rates.

Interest Rate Risk
One of the important types of risk confronting investors, resulting from a rise in interest rates.

Intermediate-Term Bond Fund
A bond fund that concentrates its portfolio in intermediate-term bonds. According to Morningstar, such funds focus on bonds with maturities between four and 10 years.

International Fund
A fund that invests in securities markets outside the U.S.

Inventory
The raw materials, work-in-progress and finished goods of a company.

Inventory Turnover
A measurement of efficiency, found by dividing the cost of goods sold for a period by average inventory at cost for the same period.

Invested Capital
Same as capital structure.

Investment Advisor
The company that manages a fund's portfolio, making the portfolio buy and sell decisions in an effort to carry out the fund's investment objective. The investment advisor is also known as the management company.

Investment Advisory Fee
The fee charged by the investment adviser or management company for managing a fund's investments.

Investment Club
A group of investors who work together, either as a formal legal partnership or as a more informal study group, to research, select and potentially purchase investments.

Investment Grade Bond
Bonds that are judged likely to maintain interest and principal payments to investors.

Investment Objective
The financial goal pursued by an investor or mutual fund manager.

Investment Philosophy
A set of values or guidelines an investor or investment club strives to follow when selecting investments.

Investment Style
The direction a fund manager pursues to achieve a fund's investment goals.

Investment Sub-advisor
A management company hired by the fund's investment advisor to manage the fund.

IRA
Abbreviation for Individual Retirement Account.

Junk Bonds
A bond considered by a credit-rating agency to be less likely to repay investors' principal or to pay interest than investment grade bonds.

Junk Bond Fund
A bond fund with a portfolio of non-investment grade bonds that pays a high interest rate compared to other bond funds. High-yield bond funds are also known as junk bond funds.

LIFO
Abbreviation for last in, first out, a method of inventory valuation.

Large Cap
With market capitalization measured by a company's sales revenue, large-cap companies are those with annual revenue greater than $4 billion.

Large-Cap Mutual Fund
A mutual fund that has a portfolio primarily composed of large-cap companies. According to the NAIC Mutual Fund Resource Center, large-cap funds primarily hold companies with a market capitalization of more than $4 billion. According to Morningstar, such a fund has a weighted market cap within the top 5 percent of the 5,000 U.S. stocks.

Lehman Brothers Aggregate Bond Index
Morningstar's benchmark for all bond funds, this index attempts to replicate the performance of the entire U.S. investment grade bond market.

Level Load
A sales fee charged to shareholders annually.

Level Load Mutual Fund
A mutual fund that charges a sales fee to shareholders annually.

Leverage
The use of debt capital in the hope of increasing the return on equity for shareholders.

Liabilities
The sum that a company or mutual fund owes it creditors.

Lien
A claim of a creditor against property of a company.

Life Cycle Fund
A fund that invests its assets in other mutual funds that are built around a particular date, such as college education or retirement.

Limited Liability
Restriction of liability to the amount invested.

Liquid Assets
Current assets that can be quickly converted into cash.

Liquidating Value
In an investment club, the total number of valuation units multiplied by the dollar value per unit. The current market value of the club.

Liquidity
The ease with which a company's assets can be converted into cash.

Listed Security
A security that has met the requirements for trading on one or more of the nation's stock exchanges.

Load
A sales charge or commission assessed by some mutual funds.

Load Mutual Fund
A mutual fund that assesses a sales charge or commission.

Long-Term Bond Fund
A bond fund that concentrates its portfolio in long-term bonds. Morningstar classifies long-term bond funds as those that focus on bonds with maturities of 10 years or more.

Long-Term Capital Gains or Losses
Realized gains or losses on securities held for more than one year.

Long-Term Debt
On the balance sheet, borrowed funds that are due for payment after one year, usually over several years.

Long-Term Liabilities
Obligations that fall due after one year, including long-term debt, deferred income taxes and deferred credits.

Low-Cost Investment Plan
A service from NAIC through which investors may purchase, for a minimal fee, the initial shares of stock necessary to enroll in a Dividend Reinvestment Plan (DRIP).

Low Credit Quality
Securities issued by a government or corporation that may not repay interest or principal to bond investors.

Lower of Cost or Market
A conservative rule of accounting that prices an item at the lower of its current market value or the price paid for it.

Management Fee
The amount that a mutual fund pays to the management company or investment advisor. It is expressed as a percentage of a fund's assets.

Management Team
A number of managers that run a mutual fund, using a team management approach.

Market Capitalization
A measure of a company's size, based on its level of annual revenue.

Market Crash
An abrupt steep decline in a well-known market benchmark that affects many of the stocks in an exchange.

Market Expansion
Expanding the markets for a company's products by increasing sales in other regions of the United States from where the company is located or even overseas.

Market Maker
A company that matches stock buy and sell orders and ensures that an orderly market is maintained in certain companies on the stock exchange.

Market Price
The price at which transactions in a security take place.

Market Sector
A particular area or portion of the stock market. Fund portfolios are analyzed by sector by both Value Line and Morningstar. Each fund-tracker divides the market into 10 nearly identical sectors.

Market Timing
A strategy used by an investor, fund manager or market speculator who hopes to buy low and sell high by darting in and out of the market.

Market Value
The sale price of an asset on the open market.

Maturities
The point in time when a bond issuer will return the money investors used to purchase a bond. Bonds are classified depending on their maturity as short, intermediate or long-term bonds.

Merchandise Turnover
The same as inventory turnover.

Mid Cap
With market capitalization measured by a company's sales revenue, mid-cap companies are those with annual revenue between $400 million and $4 billion.

Mid-Cap Mutual Fund
A mutual fund that has a portfolio primarily composed of mid-cap companies. According to Morningstar, a mid-cap fund has a portfolio with a weighted median market capitalization of between 80 to 95 percent of the 5,000 largest U.S. stocks. According to the NAIC Mutual Fund Resource Center, a mid-cap fund holds companies with a market capitalization between $400 million and $4 billion.

Minimum Purchase Amounts
The lowest investment a mutual fund requires for an investor to open an account.

Money Market Account
A type of mutual fund that invests in cash equivalents and whose net asset value is almost always $1.00.

Money Market Fund
These funds invest in safe, highly liquid, short-term securities with maturities of 90 days or less. They pay interest on their investments to shareholders.

Money Market Instruments
Money market instruments are short-term securities with maturities of 90 days or less. These instruments are held by money market funds.

Morgan Stanley European, Australian & Far East Index (EAFE)
An index created and managed by Morgan Stanley Dean Whitter that is composed of companies in Europe, Australia and the Far East.

Morgan Stanley World Index
An index created and managed by Morgan Stanley Dean Whitter that contains companies from all countries with stock markets around the world weighted by their market capitalization.

Morningstar
An investment education company that issues data reports on mutual funds. Morningstar reports are widely available in public libraries.

Mortgage
A loan to finance the purchase of real estate, one form of long-term debt on the balance sheet.

Mortgage Backed Securities
A security that represents ownership of an interest in a group of mortgages.

Multiple
Another term for price/earning ratio.

Municipal Bond
A bond issued by a state, city or local government or local governmental agency. The interest payable by these bonds is not subject to federal taxes. Some municipal bonds are free of state and local taxes as well.

Municipal Bond Fund
A bond fund that holds municipal bonds.

Mutual Fund
An open-end investment company that buys back or redeems its shares on command at their current net asset value.

Mutual Fund Company
These companies are structured as corporations or businesses trusts and supervised by a board of directors. Mutual fund companies generally outsource their various functions to investment advisors, distributors, custodians and transfer agents.

Mutual Fund Check List
A study tool developed by NAIC that enables you to evaluate the key elements of a mutual fund: its portfolio, management record and expenses.

Mutual Fund Comparison Guide
A study tool developed by NAIC that enables you to compare the key elements of stock (equity) mutual funds to one another. This tool can be used to compare different fund categories as well.

Mutual Fund Trend Report
A study tool developed by NAIC that allows you to track a single fund to see if changes have been made in the fund's portfolio, management record and expenses over time.

NAIC Forum on CompuServe
An online gathering place where NAIC members participate in investment-related discussions and education.

Nasdaq 100
An index of the largest and most actively traded non-financial companies listed in the Nasdaq National Market, heavily weighted towards technology and telecommunications companies.

New Fund
A mutual fund with no history, newly offered to the investing community.

New Technology
A technology that makes a substantial improvement in a manufacturing, communications or other process. New technology can be an important source of a company's growth.

Net Asset Value
The market value of a fund's assets, less any liabilities and fund expenses, divided by the number of shares outstanding.

Net Income Before Taxes (Pre-Tax Profit)
Earnings or income before taxes.

Net Income After Taxes (Profit or Earnings)
Profit or earnings after taxes.

Net Interest Margin
The profit margin for financial institutions, found by dividing net interest revenues by average earning assets.

Net Sales
Gross sales minus returns and allowances.

Net Working Capital
The difference between current assets and current liabilities.

Net Worth
All assets minus all liabilities of a corporation. Net worth is equivalent to stock, paid-in capital and retained earnings.

New York Stock Exchange
The largest auction market securities exchange in the nation.

No-Load Mutual Fund
A commission-free mutual fund.

Nominal Return
The actual rate of return not adjusted for inflation, contrasted with real returns.

Non-Investment Grade Bond
A bond considered by a credit rating agency to be less likely to pay interest or repay principal to bond investors than an investment grade bond. Standard & Poor's considers bonds rated BBB or below to be non-investment grade; Moody's considers bonds rated Baa or below to be non-investment grade.

Non-Operating Income and Expense
Income and expense of a corporation not connected with the principal business. Sale of property is an example of non-operating income; payment of interest to bondholders is an example of non-operating expense.

Notes Payable
A current liability on the balance sheet for money owed. usually to a bank by a company, as evidenced by promissory notes.

Odd Lot
Less than a round lot, which is the established unit of trading in a security. For most issues, from one to ninety-nine shares constitutes an odd lot.

Off-Board Security
Same as unlisted or over-the-counter security. A security not listed on a stock exchange.

Online Broker
A broker that primarily does business on the Internet.

Online Premium Services (OPS)
NAIC membership benefit that includes downloadable stock selection data and BITS, the NAIC online newsletter.

Open-End Fund
A fund that will redeem shares for cash or issue new shares.

Operating Expenses
Generally defined as selling, general and administrative expense.

Operating Profit
Gross profit minus operating expenses.

Operating Ratio
A measurement of efficiency, calculated as cost of goods sold, plus selling, general and administrative expenses, divided by net sales.

Options
Contracts that give the buyer the right, but not the obligation, to buy or sell a futures contract or a specified quantity of a commodity, security, currency or index at a specific price within a specified period of time, regardless of the current market price of the underlying item.

Ordinary Income Rate
The rate at which the Federal government taxes a particular level of earned income.

Other (Non-Operating) Income
Income of a corporation not connected with the principal business. Sale of property is an example of non-operating income.

Other (Non-Operating) Expense
Expense of a corporation not connected with the principal business. Payment of interest to bond-holders is an example of non-operating expense.

Outstanding Stock
Stock issued and in the hands of owners.

Overhead
Similar to Fixed Costs.

Over-the-Counter Market (OTC)
Marketplace for securities that, because the issuing companies cannot qualify or do not care to do so, are not listed on any securities exchange.

P/E Ratio
The price/earnings ratio (P/E) is determined by dividing a stock's market price by its earnings per share. For a mutual fund, the fund's average P/E ratio is the average P/E ratio of all the companies held in the portfolio. The P/E ratio is used to determine if a stock represents value at a given price. The market generally accords higher P/E ratios to companies growing at higher-than-average rates.

PERT
Portfolio Evaluation Review Technique, an NAIC tool permitting investors to keep current on the latest figures on their holdings and to take action as appropriate.

Paid-In Capital
Capital arising from payments by stockholders, in contrast to earned surplus, which arises from profits.

Partnership Agreement
A legal document signed by members of an investment club that establishes and defines their formal organization as a partnership.

Passive Investment Management
Management that relies on diversification to represent a broad-based market index, without using special strategies or information to attempt to achieve better results than the market index.

Patents
An invention or discovery that is protected by law from being duplicated by competitors.

Pay-Out Ratio
The ratio of cash dividends to net earnings.

Percent Earned on Equity
Net earnings divided by shareholders' equity.

Performance
The total return of a mutual fund during a particular period of time.

Pink Sheets
Report available at brokerage offices that lists current prices for less popular over-the-counter stocks whose worth is not reported in the newspaper.

Plant Turnover
Same as fixed asset turnover.

Portfolio
All of the securities held by a mutual fund.

Portfolio Earnings Growth Rate
A measure of the annualized earnings growth rate of a stock fund's portfolio over a certain period of time. Morningstar provides this for the most recent three years, while Value Line provides this figure for the most recent five years.

Portfolio Management
The maintenance, buying and selling decisions an investor makes regarding his or her investments.

Portfolio Management Guide
An NAIC tool permitting users to keep watch over the price movement of their holdings.

Portfolio Manager
The individual or individuals responsible for the management of a mutual fund—that is, for the holding, buying and selling of securities in a fund portfolio.

Preferred Stock
An equity security that pays shareholders a dividend at a specified rate.

Preferred Stock Ratio
That portion of a company's capital structure consisting of preferred stock.

Prepaid Expense
An asset representing an advance payment, generally for services and supplies, classified as current on the balance sheet.

Prepayment
Paying a debt obligation before the due date. Bonds with prepayment terms are also known as callable bonds.

Pre-Tax Profit
Earnings or income before taxes.

Pre-Tax Profit Margin
Profit before taxes divided by sales.

Price Appreciation
The advance in price of a security.

Price/Earnings (P/E) Ratio
The market price of a security divided by the earnings per share. Used to determine if a stock represents value at a given price.

Principal
The original sum of money invested as capital.

Privately Held
A company that is owned privately. Privately held companies do not issue stock on the stock exchanges, thus are not available as investing vehicles for individual or institutional investors.

Pro Forma
A financial statement that was made to reflect a proposed change, such as a merger or acquisition.

Profit
The positive gain from an investment or business. Same as earnings or income.

Profit and Loss Statement
Same as earning report.

Prospectus
A written document offering to sell securities, which provides information required by the Securities and Exchange Commission. The prospectus describes the fund's objectives, strategies, risks, fees and expenses. It also describes the funds policies regarding buying, redeeming, reinvesting and exchanging fund shares.

Proxy
A document seeking shareholder approval for some fund action or activity.

Publicly Held
A company that has stock available for sale on a stock exchange. Individual and institutional investors can invest in publicly held corporations.

Purchasing Power Risk
The risk of loss in the value of cash due to inflation, one of the important types of risks confronting investors.

Quality
A rating given to bonds and stocks by a recognized rating service.

Quality Company (Stock)
A company that has had five-10 years of consistent increases in sales and earnings, and has also consistently maintained superior pre-tax profit margins and earnings on invested capital.

Quarterly Report
A report issued by a mutual fund detailing a fund's performance, expenses and holdings during a particular three months. The quarterly report also contains the fund manager's letter regarding the fund's performance during the past three months as well as overall economic conditions.

Quick Asset
A current asset readily converted into cash.

Quick Asset Ratio
Same as acid test ratio.

REIT (Real Estate Investment Trust)
A company that buys and manages real estate investments and whose shares sell on the stock market.

Ratio Analysis
The use of mathematical ratios in analyzing the performance of a company and its industry.

Ratio Chart
A graph, such as the one on the NAIC Stock Selection Guide, which depicts relative changes or geometric progressions. A ratio chart is used to plot rates of growth in sales and earnings.

Real Return
The rate of return of an investment adjusted for inflation.

Receipts
Same as sales and revenues.

Receivables
A current asset representing amounts owed to a company that are to be collected within the next year.

Redemption Fee
A fee charged by some funds for selling fund shares before a certain period of time.

Refunding
Replacing one bond issue with another of a lower rate when it is to the financial advantage of the corporation to do so.

Registrar
The agent, usually a bank or trust company, responsible for issuing and distributing shares of stock and bonds.

Regular Trading Day
The markets are regularly open from 9:30 a.m. to 4 p.m., Monday through Friday, except for Federal holidays.

Reinvest
To put back a sum of money into a particular investment that an investor has obtained, such as a stock or mutual fund dividend or capital gains distribution.

Relative Value
For NAIC investors, the current price/earnings ratio (based on EPS for the latest twelve months) as a percent of the historical average price/earnings ratio.

Repurchase Agreement
Short-term agreements under which a dealer in government securities sells such a security to an investor and purchases it back the next day. Bond funds may invest in repurchase agreements.

Researcher
A mutual fund adviser employee who researches companies for possible purchase.

Retained Earnings
Money a company keeps from net profits in order to finance its future operations.

Retained Income
Same as retained earnings.

Return
A measure of performance usually based on the profit per dollar invested.

Return on Book
Percent earned on book value, or return on equity.

Revenues (Sales)
Synonymous with sales and receipts.

Reverse Split
A decrease in a company's shares outstanding. Investors in the company end up with more stock, worth more per share, but their stock doesn't actually increase or decrease in value.

Reward
A satisfying return or result. A profit.

Risk
The possibility of suffering a financial loss on an investment.

Risk Capital
Refers to the nature of money that should be invested in the stock market, funds not earmarked for specific near-term purposes.

Roth IRA
A tax-deferred Individual Retirement Account in which an investor makes a taxable contribution and the money is not taxed when withdrawn after retirement.

Round Lot
The established unit of trading in a security, usually 100 shares.

Rule of Five
A rule for investors stating that for every five stocks purchased, one will experience unforeseen difficulties, three will perform more or less as expected, and one will far exceed what was forecast for it.

Russell 2000
An index of small company stocks created and managed by Russell. Fund managers who manage small-cap mutual funds use the Russell 2000 index as a benchmark to measure their fund's performance.

Russell 3000
An index that measures the 3000 most actively traded U.S. companies by market capitalization. It is a measure of total stock market performance. This index is a reflection of broad stock market performance and can be used as a benchmark for U.S. growth stock funds.

S&P 500 Index
A measure of the performance of 400 industrial stocks, 20 transportation stocks, 40 financial stocks and 40 public utilities in the United States, selected by a committee at Standard & Poor's. Commonly used as a performance benchmark by mutual funds.

Sales (Revenues)
The amount received by a company from the selling of its products and services.

Sales Charges
A load or commission assessed by some mutual funds.

Sales Commission
A fee paid by investors in return for financial advice. Brokers and financial planners receive a sales commission in return for selling their clients mutual funds.

Sales Growth
The rate of increase in a company's sales growth during the past four years.

Section 529 Plan
State-sponsored college savings plan.

Sector Fund
A fund that concentrates its portfolio on a specialized industry sector.

Securities
Stocks, bonds or other instruments that investors can own and trade on financial markets.

Securities and Exchange Commission (SEC)
The federal agency that regulates the securities business and protects the interests of the investing public.

Sell Zone
On NAIC forms, that range of calculated prices indicating that the holding is a candidate for sale.

Selling, General & Administrative Expenses
Non-manufacturing expenses such as salaries of executives, commissions paid to salespeople, and advertising and public relations outlays.

Semi-Annual Report
A report issued by a mutual fund detailing a fund's performance, expenses and holdings during a particular six months. The semi-annual report also contains the fund manager's letter regarding the fund's performance during the six months as well as overall economic conditions.

Semi-log Chart
A chart such as the one used in the Visual Analysis section of the NAIC Stock Selection Guide, where the vertical scale is based on logarithms.

Share Classes
Many fund companies offer funds in different share classes. These are most often funds with different types of loads, or funds with varying investment minimums.

Shareholder
Synonymous with stockholder or shareowner, the owner of one or more shares of a corporation or mutual fund. When you become a shareholder of a corporation or mutual fund, you own a portion of the companies in the fund's portfolio.

Shareholder Redemptions
Shareholders who sell their shares in an open-ended mutual fund.

Shareholders' Equity
Same as equity.

Shares Outstanding
The number of shares issued by a company available to the investing public.

Shareholder Report
A periodic report issued by a mutual fund company about a fund containing the fund manager's update, fund performance statistics and a list of portfolio holdings.

Short-Term Bonds
Bonds with maturity dates between one and four years according to fund tracker Morningstar, and less than three years according to Value Line. Short-term bonds and short-term bond funds are less subject to interest rate swings and are somewhat less volatile than long-term bonds and bond funds.

Short-Term Bond Fund
A fund that invests primarily in bonds with maturity dates between one and four years, as defined by Morningstar.

Short-Term Capital Gains or Losses
Realized gains or losses on securities held one year or less.

Short-Term Global Income Funds
Funds with portfolios that hold short-term bonds from different countries around the world, including the United States.

Short-Term Securities
Bonds that mature in three-and-a-half years or less.

Single State Municipal Bond Funds
Funds that have portfolios composed of Single State Municipal Bond Funds or governmental agencies within a single state.

Sliding Scale
A fee or charge that is reduced gradually depending on certain factors, such as time or income.

Small Cap
With market capitalization measured by a company's sales revenue, small-cap companies are those with annual revenue less than $400 million.

Small-Cap Mutual Fund
A mutual fund that has a portfolio primarily composed of small-cap companies. According to the NAIC Mutual Fund Resource Center, small-cap funds primarily hold companies with a market capitalization of less than $400 million. According to Morningstar, such funds have portfolios with a weighted median market capitalization of the bottom 80 percent of the 5,000 largest U.S. stocks.

Socially-Responsible Investor
An investor whose investment strategy includes choices based on social or political beliefs.

Soft Money
A practice by which a mutual fund obtains analysts reports and company information in return for directing brokerage trades to a specific broker.

Solvency
Measure of a company's ability to meet its long-term debt obligations.

Special Securities
Complex or illiquid securities outside of the ordinary range of investments for a mutual fund.

Spread
The difference between a security's bid and asked prices.

Statement of Additional Information
This document provides data about the corporate aspects of a fund and its advisors. It also includes financial statements and fund director biographies.

Stock (Common)
A unit of ownership of a public corporation.

Stock Check List (SCL)
An NAIC form to be used until the investor has gained mastery of the Stock Selection Guide.

Stock Comparison Guide (SCG)
An NAIC form designed to assist investors in comparing two or more securities before making a purchase decision.

Stock Dividend
Distribution of stock to shareholders as a dividend on shares held.

Stock Exchanges
A physical place or electronic platform where stocks are traded. Major U.S. exchanges include the New York Stock Exchange, NASDAQ and the American Stock Exchange.

Stock Fund
A mutual fund that has a portfolio primarily composed of stock. Also known as an equity fund.

Stock Index Futures
An agreement from an investor to buy or sell a set amount of a stock index at a certain price by a certain date.

Stock Selection Guide & Report
An NAIC form designed to assist investors in making a judgment about whether or not to buy a security.

Stock Split
An increase or decrease in a company's outstanding shares. In a traditional split, a company increases its shares outstanding and the value of its stock is reduced accordingly. In a reverse split, the shares outstanding are reduced, increasing the value of the stock.

Stockholder
Synonymous with shareholder, the owner of one or more shares of a corporation.

Straight-Line Depreciation
A depreciation method in which the same amount is deducted every year.

Street Name
Refers to securities held in the name of the broker rather than the customer.

Sub-Advisor
A management company hired by a fund's investment advisor to manage a fund.

Sub-Adviser Fees
The fee charged by the investment sub-adviser for managing a fund's investments.

Sub-Sector Fund
A fund that specializes in a sub-category of a particular market sector. For example, a telecommunications fund is a technology sub-sector fund.

Sum of the Years' Digits
A form of accelerated depreciation.

Systematic Withdrawal Plans
Programs offered by some mutual funds that allow shareholders to receive regular payments from their investments.

Tax-Adjusted Return
A fund's annualized after-tax total return for a certain time period.

Tax-Deferred
A characteristic of certain investment accounts that allows contributions and earnings to be made and accumulate tax-free.

Tax-Deferred Retirement Plans
Plans that allow contributions and earnings to be made and accumulate tax-free.

Tax Efficiency
A measure of a mutual fund's history in regard to fund distributions.

Tax-Exempt
Securities exempt from federal, state or local taxes.

Tax Identification Number
Form SS-4 is submitted for a partnership, and the resulting number is furnished to brokers and transfer agents. Mandatory for an investment club.

Tax Liability
Taxes owed by an individual or corporation to local, state or federal governments.

Taxable Account
Money held in such an account is subject to taxation by local, state and/or federal governments.

Taxable Bond Fund
A bond fund that invests in taxable bonds.

Thin Market
A market in which there are few offers to buy or sell a security, characteristic of stocks with a small number of shares outstanding.

Term Life Insurance
Life insurance protection that lasts a limited number of years and expires without value if the insured survives the stated period.

Total Assets
The total of the entire fund's shares at the end of the most recently reported month.

Total Return
The performance of an investment, including dividends, interest, capital gains distributions and changes in net asset value. The total return is the change in value of an investment during a given period of time.

Trader
An individual who does a good deal of buying and selling in the hope of realizing short-term profits.

Trading Desk
The offices where fund employees place securities buy and sell orders.

Trading on Equity
Same as leverage.

Traditional IRA
A tax-deferred Individual Retirement Account in which an investor makes a tax-deductible contribution and the money is taxed when withdrawn after retirement.

Trailing Portfolio Earnings Growth Rate
A measure of the annualized earnings growth rate of a stock fund's portfolio over the past four years.

Transfer Agent
A company that prepares and maintains records relating to shareholder accounts.

Transfer Agent Expenses
The fees charged by the transfer agent to the mutual fund company. The transfer agent maintains mutual fund shareholder records, keeping track of how many shares each shareholder owns. Specific costs for transfer agent activities can be found in a mutual fund's financial statements.

Treasury Bill
A U.S. government obligation that matures within a year of issuance.

Treasury Bond
A U.S. government obligation that matures more than five years from the date of issuance.

Treasury Note
A U.S. government obligation that matures from one to five years from the date of issuance.

Turnover
The volume of trading in a particular security or in the market as a whole.

Turnover Rate
A rough measure of how much buying and selling a fund manager does in a mutual fund portfolio.

12b-1 Fee
An annual charge deducted from a shareholder's assets to pay for a fund's distribution and marketing costs.

U.S. Bond Funds
Bond funds that invest their assets in bonds issued in the United States.

U.S. Stock Funds
Stock funds that invest their assets in U.S. companies.

Undistributed Earnings
Same as retained income.

Undistributed Profits
Same as retained income.

Unit Investment Trust
A basic type of investment company that issues units the Unit Investment Trust will buy back from investors at an investor's request. Unit investment trusts have unmanaged portfolios and a termination date, although that date may be many years in the future.

Unit Value System
An investment club accounting method that permits varying contributions and partial withdrawals as well as skips in contributions.

Unlisted Security
Same as an off-board security.

Unrealized Gain or Loss
A gain or loss not transacted yet (i.e. a "paper gain" or "paper loss").

Upside/Downside Ratio
On NAIC forms, a measurement of risk. Divide the upside potential by the downside risk.

Upside Potential
On NAIC forms, the difference between the calculated high price and the current price.

Valuation Statement
Investment club accounting report that lists assets at market value as of a certain date.

Value
The ability to buy a "quality" "growth" company at a low enough price that will allow you to double your money in the next five years.

Value Line
An investment education company that issues mutual fund reports and provides electronic fund information.

Value Manager
A mutual fund manager whose investment strategy is to buy shares of companies with earnings growth potential that are selling at a discount.

Value Style of Investing
Managers who follow this style buy companies that appear to be undervalued based on defined measurements such as the P/E ratio or price-to-book ratio.

Valuation Statement
Investment club accounting report that lists assets at market value as of a certain date.

Variable Cost
The expense of a corporation that varies with the amount of goods produced.

Visual Analysis
That portion of the Stock Selection Guide containing the ratio chart, where sales and earnings trend lines are established and prices recorded.

Volatility
A measurement of the change in price of a security over a given period.

Wasting Asset
An asset that is exhausted in production.

Wilshire 4500
An index of mid- and small-cap companies, which contains all publicly traded companies except those in the S&P 500.

Wilshire 5000
A value-weighted index of the most active stocks in the U.S. market. This index is a performance measure of total U.S. stock market activity.

Working Capital
The difference between current assets and current liabilities.

Working Capital Ratio
Same as current ratio.

Yield
The per-share cash dividend divided by the per-share market price of a stock or fund. Also called dividend yield.Index

Index

A

Accelerated depreciation, 160
Account maintenance fees, 160
Accounts payable, 160
Accounts receivable, 160
Accrued taxes, 160
Accrued wages/interest/other expenses, 160
Accumulated profits, 160
Acid test ratio, 160
Acquisitions, 160
Actively managed mutual fund, 46, 89, 91, 93, 98, 99, 160
Active portfolio strategy, 160
Adviser, 160
After tax return, 160
A.G. Edwards, 79
Aggressive growth fund, 103, 160
AIMR
. *See* Association for Investment **Management and Research**
American Depository Receipts (ADRs), 160
American Stock Exchange (AMEX), 58
Amortization, 160
Analyst, 160
Annual report, 105, 106, 151, 153, 160
Annuity, 52, 160
Application, 160
Ask price, 82, 160
Asset, 11, 160
   hidden, 164
Asset allocation, 41
   calculating current, 44
   definition of, 160
   importance of, 43
   managing returns, 42
   managing volatility through, 41–42
   rules for managing, 42–43
   vs. diversification, 44
Asset allocation, determining
   choosing asset class, 43
   choosing risk tolerance, 43
   goals for investment dollars, 44

length of investment horizon, 43
Asset allocation fund, 160
Association for Investment Management and Research (AIMR), 17
Authorized stock, 160
Automatic reinvestment plan (dividend reinvestment), 160
Average credit quality, 160
Average effective duration, 160
Average effective maturity, 160
Average P/E ratio, 160
Averages, 160

B

Back-end load fund, 160
Balanced fund, 102, 160
Balanced stock/bond mutual funds, risk/return on, 33
Balance sheet, 160
Bank savings account, risk/return on, 30–31
Basis, 160
Bear, 160
Beardstown Ladies' Investment Club, 119
Bear market, 22, 160
Benchmark, 40, 160
Beta, 160
Better Investing magazine, 4, 63, 64, 130, 142, 161
Better Investing National Convention, 5, 141, 161
Bid price, 82, 161
BITS, 4, 142, 161
Blend style of investing, 90, 161
Blue chip, 65, 161
Board of directors, 106, 161
Bond fund, 102, 161
   bond index fund, 161
   global, 164
   government general, 164
   government treasury, 164
   high-yield, 164
   intermediate-term, 164

international, 164
   junk, 165
   long-term, 165
   municipal, 32, 166
   short-term, 169
   single state municipal, 169
   taxable, 169
   U.S., 170
   . *See* also Bonds
Bondholder, 161
Bond index fund, 161
Bond market, average growth over 78 years, 22 (fig)–23
Bond ratings, 161
Bond ratio, 161
Bonds
   convertible, 32
   corporate, 32, 162
   corporate high yield, 162
   definition of, 161
   foreign, 163
   government, 164
   investment grade, 165
   junk, 34, 102, 165
   low quality, 34–35
   municipal, 32, 166
   non-investment grade, 166
   Series EE, 30
   Series HH, 30
   short-term, 168
   treasury, 30, 170
   . *See* also Bond fund
Book value (common stock), 161
Broker, 16, 161, 162, 166
   . *See* also Buying/selling stock
Brokerage
   brokerage scorecard Web site, 16
   commission free trade, 162
   discount, 16, 79–80, 89, 162
   full-service brokerage, 79
   online, 79–80
   other brokerage option, 81
Brokerage commission, 93, 161
Brokerage house, 161

Brokerage scorecard, Web site for, 16
Bull market, 22, 161
Business cycle, 161
BuyandHold, 81
Buy and hold philosophy, 161
Buying/selling mutual funds
    initial investments, 107
    investment options for, 106–107
    recordkeeping, 107
    tax implication of, 107
Buying/selling stock
    bid vs. ask price, 82
    cash vs. margin account, 83–84
    choosing broker, 81–82
    day vs. good-til-canceled order, 83
    declining fundamentals as reason
      to sell, 84
    discount/online brokerage, 79–80
    dividend reinvestment/direct share
      purchase plan, 80
    fraud/scandal as reason to sell, 84–85
    full-service brokerage, 79
    investment club for, 81
    limit order for, 83
    market order for, 82–83
    money need as reason to sell, 84
    NAIC Low Cost Investment Plan,
      80–81
    other brokerage option, 81
    placing order, 82
    portfolio rebalancing as reason to
      sell, 85
    retirement account and, 81
Buy zone, 161
Bylaws
    . See Club operating procedures

C

Capital appreciation, 161
Capital gain or capital loss
    definition of, 161
    long-term, 39, 165
    short-term, 39, 169
Capital gains, 39, 50, 51, 59, 106,
    107, 152
Capital gains distribution, 99, 161
Capitalism, 161
Capitalist, 161
Capitalization, 161

Capital structure, 161
Cash, 161
Cash account, 83
Cash dividend, 161
Cash flow, 42, 139, 145, 161
Cash flow statement, 161
Cash reserves, 161
Certificate of deposit (CD) risk/return
    on, 32
Certified Financial Planner (CFP), 17
CFA
    . See Chartered Financial Analyst
Challenge Club, 141
Charles Schwab, 89
Chartered Financial Analyst (CFA), 17
Chartered Financial Consultant
    (ChFC), 17
Chartered Life Underwriter (CLU), 17
Chartist, 68
Cheap stock, 161
ChFC
    . See Chartered Financial Consultant
Chief executive officer (CEO), 161
Class A shares, 161
Class B shares, 161
Class C shares, 161
Classic Plus software (NAIC), 144
Classic software (NAIC), 144–145
    (fig), 147
Closed-end investment company
    (or fund), 94, 161
CLU
    . See Chartered Life Underwriter
Club operating procedures, 122, 161
Club Treasurers List, 162
Collectibles, risk/return on, 35
College savings plan, 52
Commission, 31, 162
Commission free brokerage trade, 162
Commodity future, risk/return on, 35
Common stock, 58, 162
Common stock ratio, 162
Compounded annual return, 26, 162
Compounding, 162
CompuFest, 5, 141, 162
Consolidated statement, 162
Contingent deferred sales charge, 162
Convertible bond, risk/return on, 32
Convertible preferred stock, 162

Corporate bond, 32, 162
Corporate bond mutual fund,
    risk/return on, 32
Corporate high yield bonds, 162
Corporation, 162
Cost basis, 162
Cost of goods sold, 162
Cost of sales, 162
Country-specific fund, 162
Coupon rate, 32
Coverdell Education Savings Account
    (ESA), 53, 162
Creditor, 162
Current asset, 162
Current liability, 162
Current ratio, 162
Current yield, 162
Custodial fees, 162
Cyclical, 162
Cyclical growth stock, 162
Cyclical industry, 162

D

Day order, 83
Day vs. good-til-cancelled (GTC)
    order, 83
Debenture, 162
Deferred charge, 162
Deferred expense, 162
Deferred tax, 52, 169
Defined benefit pension, 50, 162
Defined contribution pension, 50, 162
Depletion, 162
Depreciation, 162
    accelerated, 160
    straight-line, 169
Derivatives, 35, 162
Dexheimer, Ann, 155
Dilution, 162
Direct Stock Purchase Plan (DSP),
    80, 162
Discount broker, 162
Discount brokerage, 16, 79–80, 89, 162
Distributor, 162
Diversification, 27, 162
    advantage of, 63
    vs. asset allocation, 44
Diversified portfolio, 162
Dividend, 26, 59, 162

Dividend per share, 162
Dividend Reinvestment Plan (DRIP), 4, 14, 46, 59, 80, 162
Dividend yield, 162
Dollar cost averaging, 23, 162
Dow Jones industrial average, 162
Downside risk, 162
DRIP
. *See* Dividend Reinvestment Plan

E _____

Earned surplus, 163
Earnings, 163
Earnings per share (EPS), 163
Earnings plowback, 163
Earnings report, 163
Economies of scale, 163
Education IRA
. *See* Coverdell Education Savings Account
Electronic communications network, 163
Electronic signature, 163
EPS
. *See* Earnings per share
Equity, 163
. *See also* Stock
Equity capital, 163
ETFs
. *See* Exchange traded funds
Exchange, 163
Exchange fee, 163
Exchange traded funds (ETFs), 103, 163
Ex-dividend, 163
Expense ratio, 92, 163
Expenses, 163

F _____

Family of funds, 163
Fannie Mae, 30
FDIC
. *See* Federal Deposit Insurance Company
Federal agency securities, risk/return on, 30
Federal Deposit Insurance Company (FDIC), 31
Federal Home Loan Mortgage (Freddie Mac), 30

Federal National Mortgage Association (Fannie Mae), 30
Fee-only financial planner, 17, 18, 163
FIFO, 163
Financial advisor/planner
definition of, 163
fee for, 17–18
finding, 18
major category of, 17
Financial leverage, 163
Financial planning, basics of
books for additional information on, 19
calculate net worth, 11–12
consider professional financial consultant, 17–18
exception to investing while paying off debt, 13–14
investigate brokerage houses/mutual fund families, 16
pay of credit card/high-interest debt, 12–13
prioritize financial goals, 11
purchase life/disability insurance, 15–16
question to consider before planning, 19
set aside money for emergency/planned expenses, 14–15
Financial risk, 163
Financial statement, 163
Fiscal period, 163
Fixed asset, 163
Fixed asset turnover, 163
Fixed cost, 163
Fixed income investment, 30, 41, 42, 163
Fixed interest rate, 32
Fixed liability, 163
Foreign bonds, 163
Foreign currencies, 163
Foreign stocks, 163
Form 1065, 163
Form 10-k, 163
Form 10-q, 163
Formula investing, 163
403(b) plan, 50–51, 81, 163
401(k) plan, 50–51, 81, 163
Fractional shares, 163
Freddie Mac, 30

Free enterprise, 163
Front-end load, 91, 163
Front-end load mutual fund, 163
Full service broker, 16, 79, 163
Fundamental analysis, 67
Fund asset size, 163
Funded debt, 164
Fund exchanges, 163
Funding, 164
Fund manager's letter, 163
Fund share classes, 163
Fund shares outstanding, 163
Fund statements, 164
Fund supermarkets, 164
Fund transfers, 164
Futures, 35, 164

G _____

GAAP
. *See* Generally accepted accounting principles
General Accounting Office, 164
Generally accepted accounting principles (GAAP), 61
Ginnie Mae, 30
Global bond funds, 164
Global fund, 103, 164
Good-til-cancelled (GTC) order, 83
Goodwill, 164
Governmental agency securities, 164
Government bond fund general, 164
Government bond fund treasury, 164
Government bonds, 164
Government National Mortgage Association (Ginnie Mae), 30
Government securities, 30, 164
Gross domestic product, 164
Gross profit, 164
Gross profit margin, 164
Gross sales, 164
Growth and income fund, 103, 164
Growth fund, 102–103, 160, 164
Growth manager, 164
Growth stock, 164
Growth style of investing, 164
GTC
. *See* Good-til-cancelled (GTC) order

H

The Hamilton Trust, 115
Hedge funds, 35, 164
Hidden asset, 164
High-yield bond fund, 164
Holdings, 164
Hold zone, 164
Hot tip, 164
Hybrid funds, 164

I

I-Club-List, 142, 164
Income, 164
Income fund, 164
Income return, 164
Income statement, 164
Income stock, 164
Index funds, 89, 93, 98–99, 164
Index mutual funds, 46, 51
Individual Retirement Account (IRA), 51, 89, 162, 164
Inflation, 25, 30–40, 164
Initial public offering (IPO), 57, 164
Insolvency, 164
Institutional funds, 164
Institutional investors, 164
Interest, 164
Interest rate, 32, 164
Interest rate risk, 164
International bond funds, 164
International funds, 103, 164
Inventory, 165
Inventory turnover, 165
Invested capital, 165
Investing
   to beat inflation, 25
   to become partial owner of
    corporate America, 25
   compounding, 23–24 (fig)
   focus on long term, 23–24, 24 (fig)
   fun of, 25
Investment advisor, 165
Investment advisory fee, 165
Investment club, 14, 81
Beardstown Ladies' Investment Club, 119
   companionship benefit of, 116
   decide whether a joiner, 117
   definition of, 165

   educational benefit of, 116
   history of, 118–119
   NAIC software accounting tools, 148 (fig)–149
   overview of, 114
   self-directed, 117
   shared investment benefit of, 117
   type of, 115–116
   . *See* also Investment club, joining;
    Investment club, starting;
    Investment club, running
Investment club, joining
   club history, 123
   formal structure of, 122–123
   investment philosophy, 123
   looking for club, 120–121
   warning signs, 123
   what to look for, 122
Investment club, running
   collect membership renewals, 134
   conduct financial audit, 134
   create annual task calendar, 134
   create monthly meeting agenda, 133
   education curriculum, 135
   establish education program, 133
   key actions for, 135
   other resource for, 135
   review club operating procedures, 134
   review portfolio, 134
   tax form preparation/filing, 134
   tips for success, 135
Investment club, starting
   choosing brokerage account, 129
   choosing official club name, 127
   collecting membership dues, 130
   computer/software decisions, 129–130
   determining club operating procedures, 128
   determining monthly contribution, 127–128
   drawing up partnership agreement, 128
   finding prosecptive members, 125
   first steps in, 125
   further meetings, 130
   introducing concept at first meeting, 126–127
   making things official at second

    meeting, 126–130
   officer election, 129
   resource for, 124
   sample investors club, 131
Investment grade bond, 165
Investment objective, 90, 165
Investment philosophy, 165
Investment style, 90, 165
Investment sub-advisor, 165
Investor's Toolkit software (NAIC), 145, 146 (fig)
IRS Web site, 49, 51, 156
Isaacs, Nancy, 37

J

John Templeton, 89
Junk bond fund, 165
Junk bonds, 34, 102, 165

L

Large cap, 165
Large-cap mutual funds, 165
Large-cap stock, risk/return on, 33
Lehman Brothers Aggregate Bond Index, 165
Level load, 165
Level load mutual fund, 165
Leverage, 165
Liabilities, 11, 165
Lien, 165
Life cycle fund, 165
LIFO, 165
Limited liability, 165
Limit order, 83
Liquid assets, 165
Liquidating value, 165
Liquidity, 165
Listed security, 165
Load, 165
Load mutual fund, 99, 165
Long-term bond fund, 165
Long-term capital gains or losses, 165
Long-term debt, 165
Long-term liabilities, 165
Lottery ticket, risk/return on, 36
Low Cost Investment Plan, 4, 80–81, 143, 165
Low credit quality, 165

Lower of cost or market, 165
Low-priced/penny stock, risk/return
on, 35
Low quality bond, risk/return on, 34–35
Low quality stock, risk/return on, 34
Lynch, Peter, 26, 63

M

Management fee, 165
Management team, 165
Margin account, 84
Margin call, 84
Market capitalization, 165
Market crash, 165
Market expansion, 165
Market maker, 165
Market order, 82–83
Market price, 165
Market sector, 165
Market timing, 165
Market value, 33, 35, 165
Massachusetts Investor Trust (MIT), 89
Maturities, 166
Merchandise turnover, 166
Merrill Lynch, 79
Mid cap, 166
Mid-cap mutual funds, 166
Mid-cap stocks, risk/return on, 34
Minimum purchase amounts, 166
Money market account, 31–32, 166
Money market funds, 102, 166
Money market instruments, 166
Morgan Stanley European, Australian
& Far East Index (EAFE), 166
Morgan Stanley World Index, 166
Morningstar, 109, 166
Mortgage, 166
Mortgage backed securities, 166
Multiple, 166
Municipal bonds, 32, 166
Municipal bond fund, 32, 166
Mutual fund, 14, 166
    brokerage commissions, 93
    expense ratio, 92
    fees/expenses, 91
    history of, 88
    investment objective for, 90
    management fees/operating
        expenses, 91

net asset value calculation, 90
no-load fund, 46, 89, 91, 92, 166
overview of, 89
redemption fees, 92
structure of, 89
12b-1 fee/other expenses, 92
. See also Buying/selling, mutual
    funds; Mutual fund,
    advantage/disadvantage of;
    Mutual fund, management style;
    Mutual fund, NAIC tool for;
    Mutual fund, type of; Mutual fund
    family
Mutual fund, advantage/disadvantage of
    convenience, 97
    diversification, 97
    fund expenses/sales charges
    lack of choice, 96
    management changes, 98
    professional management, 97
    sector exposure, 97
    seems easier choice, 98
    small investment amounts, 97
    style drift, 98
    taxable events, 98–99
Mutual fund, management style
    actively managed funds, 46, 89, 91,
        93, 98, 99, 160
    closed fund, 94
    index funds, 93
    open vs. closed-end fund, 94
Mutual fund, NAIC tool for
    Better Investing Mutual Fund
    Education/Resource Center, 112 (fig)
    data source for, 109
    filling out form, 109
    overview of, 108
    Stock Fund Check List, 69, 70
        (fig)–71 (fig), 110 (fig), 145, 169
    Stock Fund Comparison Guide, 76
        (fig)–77, 110 (fig), 144
    Stock Fund Trend Report, 110–111
        (fig)
    using Morningstar report, 109
Mutual fund, type of
    aggressive growth fund, 103
    balanced fund, 102
    bond fund, 102
    exchange traded fund, 103
    global fund, 103

growth fund, 102–103
growth/income fund, 103
international fund, 103
money market fund, 102
Real Estate Investment Trust
    (REIT) fund, 103
relative risk pyramid for mutual
    fund, 101 (fig)
sector fund, 103
stock fund, 102
stock income fund, 103
Mutual fund check list, 166
Mutual fund company, 166
Mutual fund comparison guide, 166
Mutual fund family
    overview of, 104–105
    prospectus for, 105–106
    shareholder report for, 106
    Statement of Additional
        Information for, 106
Mutual fund family/brokerage, 31
Mutual fund trend report, 166

N

NAIC Club Accounting (NCA)
    software, 148 (fig), 149
NAIC Forum on CompuServe,
    141–142 (fig), 166
NAIC Investment Club Partnership
    Agreement (sample), 157–159
NAIC investment principle/guideline
    define investment philosophy, 44–45
    diversify portfolio, 6, 27, 95
    do own research, 46–47
    hold for long term, 47
    invest in quality growth company,
        6, 26, 95
    invest regularly, 6, 26, 94–95
    keep expenses low, 46
    reinvest earnings/dividends/profits,
        6, 26 (fig), 95
    stick to one strategy, 45–46
NAIC Low Cost Investment Plan, 46, 64
NAIC (National Association of
    Investors Corporation)
    advantage of early investing, 2
    classes/national events, 5
    history of, 7
    how to use present book, 4

investment principles (See NAIC investment principle/guideline)

membership benefits, 4–5

mission of, 1

overview of NAIC investing books, 3

overview of present book, 3

personalized learning, 5

rewards of investing, 6

toll free number for, 126

vision of, 1

as voice for small investor, 5

NAIC Online Club Accounting (NOCA) software, 148, 149 (fig)

NAIC Rule of Five, 47

NAIC software

Classic, 144

Classic Plus, 144

investment club accounting tools, 148 (fig)–149

portfolio management tools, 147

Portfolio Record Keeper (PRK), 40, 41 (fig), 147–148 (fig), 153 (fig)

stock analysis tool, 144

Stock Analyst PLUS!, 145–146 (fig)

Stock Prospector, 65, 146–147 (fig)

NAIC Stock Prospector software, 65, 146–147 (fig)

NAIC Web site, 112

Better Investing archives, 142

Club Treasurer's List online, 140 (fig)

creating community through, 139

Education link, 142

home page, 139 (fig)

I-Club-List, 139–140, 142

Low Cost Investment Plan, 143

NAIC Forum on CompuServe, 141–142 (fig), 166

Online Premium Service, 143 (fig)

Online Store, 143

regional chapter list, 140

special interest list, 140–141

NASD

. See National Association of Securities Dealers

National Association of Securities Dealers Automated Quotes (NASDAQ), 17, 100, 166

Net asset value (NAV), 90, 166

Net income after taxes (profit or earnings), 166

Net income before taxes (pre-tax profit), 166

Net interest margin, 166

Net sales, 166

Net working capital, 166

Net worth, 11–12, 166

New fund, 166

New technology, 166

New York Stock Exchange (NYSE), 58, 166

Nicholson, George A., Jr., 7, 69

No-load mutual fund, 46, 89, 91, 92, 166

Nominal return, 39, 166

Non-investment grade bond, 166

Non-operating income and expense, 166

Notes payable, 166

O

Odd lot, 60, 166

Off-board security, 166

Online broker, 166

Online brokerage, 79–80

Online Investors School, 142

Online Premium Services (OPS), 4, 68, 130, 143 (fig), 144, 166

Online resource guide, 156

Open-end fund, 94, 166

Open-end mutual fund, 89

Operating expenses, 166

Operating profit, 166

Operating ratio, 167

Options, 35, 167

Ordinary income rate, 107, 167

OTC

. See Over-the-counter market

Other (non-operating) expense, 167

Other (non-operating) income, 167

Outstanding stock, 167

Overhead, 167

Over-the-counter market (OTC), 58, 167

P

Paid-in capital, 167

Partnership agreement, 118, 167

Passive investment management, 89, 93, 167

Patents, 167

Pay-out ratio, 167

P/E ratio

. See Price to earnings (P/E) ratio

Percent earned on equity, 167

Performance, 167

PERT

. See Portfolio Evaluation and Review Technique

Pink sheets, 167

Pioneers On-Line Investment Club (POLIC), 141

Plant turnover, 167

POLIC

. See Pioneers On-Line Investment Club

Portfolio

definition of, 167

diversification of, 6, 27, 95

high turnover, 99

managing, 167

portfolio earnings growth rate, 167

portfolio managing, 167

portfolio rebalancing, 85

tracking, 153

trailing portfolio earnings growth rate, 170

Portfolio Evaluation and Review Technique (PERT), 144, 145, 167

Portfolio management, 167

Portfolio Management Guide, 144, 167

Portfolio manager, 167

Portfolio Record Keeper (PRK) software, 40, 41 (fig), 147–148 (fig), 153 (fig)

Preferred stock

definition of, 167

risk/return on, 33

vs. common stock, 58

Preferred stock ratio, 167

Prepaid expense, 167

Prepayment, 167

Pre-tax profit, 167

Pre-tax profit margin, 167

Price appreciation, 167

Price to earnings (P/E) ratio, 61, 72, 77, 160, 167

Principal, 31, 167

Privately held, 167

PRK

. See Portfolio Record Keeper

Profit, 167

Profit and loss statement, 167
Pro forma, 167
Prospectus, 89, 167
Proxy, 167
Publicly held, 167
Purchasing power risk, 167

Q

Quality, 167
Quality company (stock), 167
Quarterly report, 153, 167
Quick asset, 167
Quick asset ratio, 167

R

Rate of return, fixed, 30
Ratio analysis, 167
Ratio chart, 168
Real estate, risk/return on, 33
Real Estate Investment Trust (REIT),
    33–34, 103, 167
Real return, 39–40, 168
Receipts, 168
Receivables, 168
Redemption fee, 92, 99, 168
Refunding, 168
Registered Representatives, 17
Registrar, 168
Regular trading day, 168
Reinvest, 168
REIT
    . See Real Estate Investment Trust
Relative risk pyramid for mutual fund,
    101 (fig)
Relative value, 168
Repurchase agreement, 168
Researcher, 168
Responsible investing
    annual to-do list, 151
    discarding quarterly/annual report,
        153
    key traits of responsible investor, 154
    monthly to-do list, 151
    recordkeeping overview, 152
    retain annual statements, 152
    retain transaction/dividend reports,
        152
    shredding monthly statement, 152
    track portfolio, 153

Retained earnings, 168
Retained income, 168
Retirement plan, employer matching, 13
Return, 21
    calculating, 40
    commission costs/expenses, 39
    definition of, 168
    inflation and, 39–40
    managing returns, 42
    nominal vs. real, 39, 40 (fig)
    taxes and, 39
    . See also Asset allocation
Return on book, 168
Reuters Investor Web site, 65
Revenues (sales), 168
Reverse split, 168
Reverse stock split, 60–61
Reward, 168
Risk, definition of, 168
Risk, level 1, lowest risk/lowest return
    bank savings accounts, 30–31
    federal agency securities, 30
    government investments, 30
    Series EE/HH bonds, 30
    treasury bills/notes/bonds, 30
Risk, level 2, low risk/low return
    certificate of deposit, 32
    high quality corporate bond/
        corporate bond mutual fund, 32
    high quality municipal bond/bond
        fund, 32
    money market account, 31–32
Risk, level 3, relatively low risk
    high quality convertible bond, 32
    high quality preferred stock, 33
Risk, level 4, intermediate risk
    balanced stock/bond mutual
        funds, 33
    large-cap stock, 33
    real estate, 33
    Real Estate Investment Trust, 33–34
Risk, level 5, relatively high risk
    collectibles, 35
    low quality bonds, 34–35
    low quality stocks, 34
    mid-cap stocks, 34
    small-cap stocks, 34
    industry mutual fund, 34

Risk, level 6, high risk
    derivatives, 35
    futures, 35
    hedge funds, 35
    lottery tickets, 36
    low-priced/penny stocks, 35
    options, 35
Risk capital, 168
Risk Pyramid, 29 (fig)
Robinson, Larry, 111
Robinson, Tristan, 111
Roth IRA, 51, 99, 168
Round lot, 60, 168
Rule of Five, 168
Russell 2000, 168
Russell 3000, 168
Russell, Frederick C., 7

S

Sales charges, 168
Sales commission, 168
Sales growth, 168
Sales (revenues), 168
Savings vs. investing, 15, 20
    reason to invest, 22–23
    risk vs. reward, 21
    short vs. long-term investing, 21–22
    . See also Investing
SCG
    . See Stock Comparison Guide
SDI
    . See Self-directed investment club
Secondary market, 57
Section 529 plan, 52–53, 168
Sector funds, 97, 103, 168
Securities, 168
Securities Act of 1933, 89
Securities and Exchange Commission
    (SEC), 57, 61, 68, 92, 121, 168
Self-directed investment club (SDI),
    117–118
Selling, general & administrative
    expenses, 168
Selling mutual funds
    . See Buying/selling mutual funds
Selling stock. See Buying/selling stock
Sell zone, 168
Semiannual report, 160
Semi-annual report, 168

Semi-log chart, 168
Series EE bonds, risk/return on, 30
Series HH bonds, risk/return on, 30
ShareBuilder, 46, 81
Share classes, 168
Shareholder, 168
Shareholder redemptions, 168
Shareholder report, 106, 168
Shareholders' equity, 168
Shares outstanding, 168
Short-term bond, 168
Short-term bond fund, 169
Short-term capital gains or losses, 169
Short-term global income funds, 169
Short-term securities, 169
Single state municipal bond funds, 169
Sliding scale, 169
Small cap, 169
Small-cap mutual fund, 169
Small-cap stocks, risk/return on, 34
Socially responsible investor, 169
Soft money, 169
Solvency, 169
Special securities, 169
Specific industry mutual fund,
    risk/return on, 34
S&P 500 index, 168
Spread, 82, 169
SSG
    . See Stock Selection Guide
Statement of Additional Information
    (SAI), 106, 169
Stock
    blue chip, 65, 161
    book value, 161
    cheap, 161
    classes of, 161
    common stock, 58, 162
    common stock ratio, 162
    convertible preferred stock, 162
    cyclical growth stock, 162
    foreign stocks, 163
    growth potential of, 58
    growth stock, 164
    income stock, 164
    initial public offering, 57
    large-cap stock, 33
    low-priced/penny stock, 35
    low quality stock, 34

mid-cap stocks, 34
outstanding stock, 167
prepared, 33, 58, 167
private vs. public company, 57
reverse stock split, 60–61
tax efficiency, 58–59
. See also Buying/selling stock;
    Stock, selecting
Stock, selecting
    with Better Investing magazine, 64
    choose industry online, 65
    choose industry without computer,
    64–65
    choose industry with software, 65
    introduction to, 62–63
    NAIC Low Cost Investment Plan, 64
    "Stock to Study," 63
    . See also Stock selection tools
Stock Analyst PLUS!, 145–146 (fig)
Stock Check List (SCL), 69, 70 (fig)–71
    (fig), 110 (fig), 145, 169
Stock (common), 169
Stock Comparison Guide (SCG), 76
    (fig)–77, 110, 144, 145, 169
Stock dividend, 169
Stock exchanges, 169
Stock fund, 102, 169
Stockholder, 169
Stock income fund, 103
Stock index futures, 169
Stock market
    average growth over 78 years, 22
    (fig)–23
    type of, 58
    Stock market terminology
    dividends, 59
    price to earnings (P/E) ratio, 61
    reverse stock split, 60–61
    Securities and Exchange
    Commission, 61
    stock split, 60
    upside/downside ratio, 61
Stock Prospector, 65, 146–147 (fig)
Stock Selection Guide (SSG), 5, 63,
    69, 72, 74 (fig)–75 (fig), 97, 144,
    145, 169
Stock selection tools
    benefit of using NAIC, 66–67
    company Web site/annual report, 69

fundamental vs. technical analysis,
    67–68
Online Premium Services, 68
overview of data source for, 67–68
Value Line/S&P, 69
Stock selection tools, NAIC
Stock Check List, 69, 70 (fig)–71
    (fig), 144
Stock Comparison Guide, 76 (fig)–77,
    110 (fig), 144, 145, 169
Stock Selection Guide, 5, 63, 69, 72,
    74 (fig)–75 (fig), 97, 144, 145, 169
Stock split, 60, 169
"Stock to Study" feature, of Better
    Investing magazine, 4, 63, 142
Straight-line depreciation, 169
Street name, 169
Sub-adviser fees, 169
Sub-advisor, 169
Sub-sector fund, 169
Sudore, Philip, 73
Sum of the years' digits, 169
Super Investors Club of Apache
    Junction, 131
Surrender charges, 52
Sweeping, 106
Systematic withdrawal plans, 169

T

T. Rowe Price, 89
Taxable account, 169
Taxable bond fund, 169
Tax-adjusted return, 99, 169
Tax-advantaged mutual fund, 99
Tax-advantaged/retirement account
    investing
    college savings plan, 52
    Coverdell Education Savings
    Account, 53
    defined contribution plan, 50–51
    employee retirement plan, 50
    individual retirement
    account/other plan, 51
    overview of, 48–49
    pre-tax retirement account, 49 (fig)
    Roth (after-tax) IRA, 51
    Section 529 plan, 52–53
    self-employed/business owner
    plan, 51

tax-deferred annuity (TDA), 52
traditional IRA, 51
Tax-deferred, 169
Tax-deferred retirement plans, 169
Tax efficiency, 169
Tax-exempt, 169
Tax identification number, 169
Tax liability, 169
Technical analysis, 67
Term life insurance, 15, 169
Thin market, 169
Total assets, 169
Total return, 169
Trader, 169
Trading desk, 169
Trading on equity, 169
Traditional IRA, 51, 169
Trailing portfolio earnings growth rate, 170
Transfer agent, 170
Transfer agent expenses, 170
Treasury bills (T-bills)
average growth over 78 years, 22 (fig)–23
definition of, 170
risk/return on, 30
Treasury bond, 30, 170
Treasury note, 30, 170
Turnover, 170
Turnover rate, 170
12b-1 fee, 92, 170

U _____

Undistributed earnings, 170
Undistributed profits, 170
Unit investment trust, 170
Unit value system, 170
Universal life insurance, 15
Unlisted security, 170
Unrealized gain or loss, 170
Upside/downside ratio, 61, 170
Upside potential, 170
U.S. bond funds, 170
U.S. stock funds, 170

V _____

Valuation statement, 170
Value, 170
Value Line, 67, 69, 109, 143, 170
Value Line Investment Survey, 64
Value manager, 170
Value style of investing, 170
Vanguard, 89, 104
Variable cost, 170
Variable interest rate, 32
Visual analysis, 170
Volatility, 21 (fig), 22, 23, 41–42, 97, 170

W _____

Wasting asset, 170
Web site
brokerage scorecard, 16
BuyandHold, 81
college savings, 156
Dividend Reinvestment Plans, 156
Financial Planning Association, 156
IRS, 49, 51, 156
National Association of Personal Financial Advisors, 156
National Association of Real Estate Investment Trusts, 156
Reuters Investor, 65
Security and Exchange Commission, 156
ShareBuilder, 81
. *See* also NAIC Web site
Whole life insurance, 15
Wilshire 4500, 170
Wilshire 5000, 170
Working capital, 170
Working capital ratio, 170
World Federation of Investment Clubs, 7

Y _____

Yield, definition of, 170

NOTES